CONSERVATORIES

CONSERVATORIES

ALAN TOOGOOD

WARD LOCK LIMITED · LONDON

© Ward Lock Limited 1987

First published in Great Britain in 1987
by Ward Lock Limited, 8 Clifford
Street, London W1X 1RB.
An Egmont Company

House editor Denis Ingram

Text filmset in Bembo by
Paul Hicks Limited
Middleton, Manchester

Printed in Portugal

British Library Cataloguing in Publication Data
Toogood, Alan R.
    1. Garden rooms   2. Indoor gardening
    I. Title
    635'.0483   SB419
    ISBN 0–7063–6512–7

Frontispiece: In this cool conservatory pelargoniums flourish, together with blue streptocarpus, orange-berried capsicums and solanums, zantedeschia (*bottom left*) and cacti and succulents. The tropical plants here, like the coloured-leaved cordylines (*centre, foreground*), would be better taken into a warm room in the house for the winter.

CONTENTS

PREFACE

Conservatories enjoyed their greatest popularity in the Victorian era, and then suffered a period of neglect. However, in recent years there has been a revival of interest in conservatories (and in lean-to greenhouses which are also used as such) and there is a wide choice available, from period to modern designs.

Conservatories today are often used as extensions of the living area. Certainly, putting up a conservatory can be a lot cheaper than moving house to gain more space, and what is more, provides an ideal environment for plants.

In this book you will find many illustrations of conservatories to help you choose one that suits the style of your house and your needs, maybe in timber or aluminium. And there is advice on equipping it, laying it out internally and landscaping the outside. I have included, too, siting the structure, planning permission and erecting it.

Conservatory plants for all-year round interest from flowers and foliage are described, with hints on their cultivation. The difficult subject of matching plants' requirements with those of people has also been covered, to enable you to choose suitable plants for living areas. I have completed my book with a chapter on caring for plants throughout the year. I hope the book gives you plenty of ideas – that is my aim.

A. T.

ACKNOWLEDGEMENTS

The publishers are especially grateful to the following persons for allowing us to photograph their conservatories: Mr & Mrs A. V. Herbert (p. 15); Mrs G. W. Williams (p. 10); Mr & Mrs A. Rees (cover, p. 18, 22 & 23); Mr & Mrs J. Matthews (p. 26); and Mr & Mrs D. Hayes (p. 2). The publishers are also grateful to The Royal Horticultural Society for allowing us to photograph a selection of plants at their Wisley garden and to the following companies for providing photographs of their conservatories: Baco Leisure Products Ltd (p. 91); & Halls Homes and Gardens Ltd (p. 87 lower). All the remaining colour photographs were taken by Bob Challinor.

All the line drawings are by Nils Solberg. Fig. 6 is after illustrations appearing in the brochure of Room Outside Ltd.

PUBLISHER'S NOTE

Readers are requested to note that in order to make the text intelligible in both hemispheres, plant flowering times, etc. are described in terms of seasons, not months. The following table provides an approximate 'translation' of seasons into months for the two hemispheres.

NORTHERN HEMISPHERE				SOUTHERN HEMISPHERE
Mid-winter	=	January	=	Mid-summer
Late winter	=	February	=	Late summer
Early spring	=	March	=	Early autumn
Mid-spring	=	April	=	Mid-autumn
Late spring	=	May	=	Late autumn
Early Summer	=	June	=	Early winter
Mid-summer	=	July	=	Mid-winter
Late summer	=	August	=	Late winter
Early autumn	=	September	=	Early spring
Mid-autumn	=	October	=	Mid-spring
Late autumn	=	November	=	Late spring
Early winter	=	December	=	Early summer

Measurements are generally cited in metric followed by the imperial equivalent in parentheses. In a few instances, owing to pressure on space, the imperial equivalent has been omitted.

CHAPTER 1

CHOICE OF MATERIALS AND BUYING

MATERIALS USED IN CONSTRUCTION

THE FRAMEWORK

We have a choice today of timber or aluminium alloy framework – that is, the glazing bars, etc, which hold the glass in place. Timber is the traditional material and there is no doubt that it blends in well with the surroundings and looks good with any style of dwelling house. Various kinds of timber are used by conservatory manufacturers, including cedarwood dressing to preserve it, but maintaining the natural colour; or primed ready for painting, white being the most popular colour for conservatories. The natural colour is 'warm' and looks particularly attractive with the older style of house.

European red pine is also used by some manufacturers and so, too, is mahogany, which is an expensive timber but has a long life.

Aluminium alloy has the advantage over timber in that it needs no preservation treatment. Many lean-to greenhouses these days are constructed of aluminium alloy, a material that blends particularly well with modern houses. One can opt for plain aluminium, or an acrylic, anodized or electrophoretic-paint finish, in bronze or white.

THE GLASS

Becoming more and more popular these days is double glazing for conservatories, which can give up to 50 % reduction in energy loss and more effective temperaure control, as well as muffling outside noise. Single glazing is still readily available, of course, and keeps down the cost of the conservatory.

Many conservatory manufacturers offer various sash designs in their modular conservatories, to match the architecture of the dwelling house. Generally toughened glass, 4 or 6 mm (0.16 or 0.24 in) thick, is used for glazing, and 7 mm (0.28 in) wire-reinforced safety glass is used by some manufacturers for the roof.

THE WALLS

The traditional conservatory is built on low walls, varying in height from 45 to 90 cm (18–36 in). Many conservatory manufacturers favour brick walls (or stone walls if it is felt these blend better with the house). However, one has a choice of timber panelling to form the walls. Many of the currently popular lean-to greenhouses have glass-to-ground level.

DOORS AND VENTILATORS

Very popular are double doors, these being side hung in most conservatories, but in lean-to greenhouses or conservatories they may be sliding. In the more expensive conservatories brass door fittings are used.

Ventilation is provided by side sashes, top or side hung, and roof ventilators, which ideally should be operated by automatic ventilator openers.

BUYING A CONSERVATORY

SPECIALIST MANUFACTURERS

There are a number of specialist conservatory manufacturers who supply modular conservatories. These companies offer an excellent service and it is best to start off by requesting their brochures which give full specifications and show plenty of examples of their conservatories. Most of these companies advertise in the gardening press, and some of them exhibit at the Chelsea Flower Show and other large horticultural shows.

There are consultants available to give customers advice on the most suitable conservatories for their requirements, the most suitable style for the house, and to assist with planning permission and building regulations.

GREENHOUSE AND CONSERVATORY MANUFACTURERS

There are many more general greenhouse and conservatory manufacturers, who supply not only free-standing greenhouses, but lean-to types which are used as conservatories or garden rooms.

Most of them advertise in the gardening press and provide fully illustrated and very informative brochures. Again it is possible to obtain advice on suitability and styles of buildings and on planning permission.

It is possible to buy on a mail-order basis from many of these companies, and generally the conservatories are supplied in kit form for DIY assembly.

DISPLAY SITES

Throughout the UK there are greenhouse display sites, often attached to garden centres, where one can see a wide range of conservatories from the general manufacturers. Not only can one compare the different makes, but also obtain advice from the site manager and his staff. Visits to your house can also generally be arranged. Manufacturers can indicate the nearest show site for their models. It does, of course, save on transport costs if you can buy from a local display site.

STAGING

Staging is necessary for displaying pot plants and there is a very wide choice available, from the simple bench type to tiered staging on which you can build up impressive displays of plants. Staging is available in timber, such as western red cedar, or in aluminium, to match the framework of the conservatory.

There is a trend today towards 'flexible' staging that can be easily dismantled and re-arranged if you want to alter the layout of your conservatory. This type of staging is in aluminium, as timber staging does not readily lend itself to re-arrangement.

Much of this flexible staging consists of tubular aluminium framework fitted together with nylon joints. Shelving bars, often

Curved eaves are a feature of many modern conservatories. This aluminium-framed model is the Eden Continental, fitted with curved glass. A major feature of this model is that it lets in plenty of light and is therefore ideally suited to plants as well as people. Size: 3.8 × 2.2 m (12½ × 7½ ft).

adjustable for various levels, hold plastic or aluminium capillary watering trays and/or slatted timber or aluminium shelves. Often you can build up, out and along as required by adding more sections, as extension packs are available. There is also special orchid-growing staging, supplied with aluminium slats on which to stand the pots, with water trays below them to provide humidity.

AUTOMATIC VENTILATOR OPENERS
There is no need to be on hand all day to open and close ventilators, for there is a wide range of automatic ventilator openers available, all very modestly priced (Fig. 1). There are versions suitable for hinged ventilators and for louvre ventilators. It is virtually essential to have automatic openers in the roof as normally this is rather too high to reach easily.

No power source is needed as these openers are powered by natural heat. The openers automatically open and close the ventilators according to the temperature changes and can be pre-set to open at a required temperature.

SHADING BLINDS
It is essential to have some form of shading to protect plants and people

The bronze finish of this Florada conservatory, 2.4 × 2.4 m (8 × 8 ft), blends beautifully with the house.

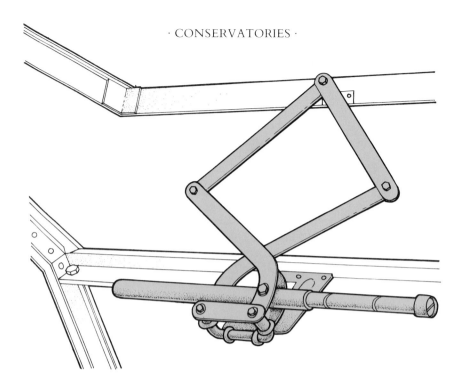

Fig. 1 These days there is no need to open and close ventilators by hand as there are automatic ventilator openers available for very reasonable prices. They can be pre-set to open when the temperature exceeds the desired level, and they close the vents again when the temperature drops. An electricity supply is not required as they are powered by natural heat.

from strong sunshine. Roller blinds constitute the most suitable system for conservatories. There are many manually operated blinds available and you will find most greenhouse manufacturers supply them.

Blinds are available in various materials, such as wooden laths, plastic reeds, shading netting, woven polyethylene, white polythene film, polypropylene netting and polyester material. However, there is no need to be on hand all day to raise and lower blinds (Fig. 2) as there are automatic systems available, and I would strongly recommend one of these as shade is provided only when it is needed.

There is a company in the UK who supply automatic, external, cedar-lath blinds. The laths are 2.5 cm (1 in) wide and 6 mm (¼ in) thick. The length and breadth of the roller blinds are made to suit individual conservatories and they can go down to ground level if required. The blinds are mounted on raised runners so that they do not interfere with ventilators.

The winding system is an electric motor controlled by adjustable

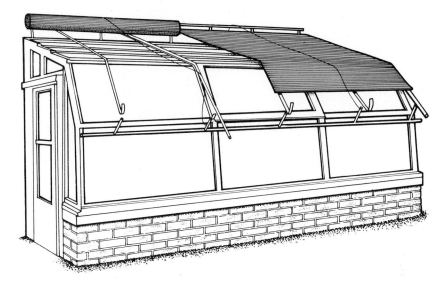

Fig. 2 Some form of shading is absolutely essential, both for plants and people, in periods of strong sunshine. There are many kinds of roller blinds to choose from, both internal and external. These are slatted wooden lath blinds, manually operated, although automatic systems are also available.

electronic thermostat and light sensors. Shade is provided only when the light intensity and the temperature in the conservatory have reached their respective selected levels. Should either one of these controlling elements decrease below the critical level the blinds will be raised.

Another UK company supplies non-retractable aluminium louvre blinds for internal or external use. The white, perforated louvres can be tilted to any angle to exclude direct sunlight. Even when the blinds are fully closed the perforations allow a certain amount of filtered light to enter the conservatory. Fitted internally in a warm or tropical conservatory, the blinds will control light only, but fitted on the outside of a cool conservatory they will help to control light and heat. There are several controls available – electric with remote switch; solar control, fully automatic with manual override; gearbox with hand-wheel or detachable handle.

AUTOMATIC WATERING
If you are away for quite a lot of the time you may find an automatic watering system useful. There are several systems available which run from the mains water supply via a header tank fitted with a ballcock valve. For large pots and containers there are various trickle and drip systems available, the water being applied via a system of spaghetti-like

Fig. 3 During the spring and summer the watering of pot plants can take up a great deal of time. An automatic watering system could therefore be considered, and is particularly useful for those people who are out all day. A capillary system, as shown here, is ideal for small pots on the staging. The pots are stood on capillary matting, which is kept moist by means of a header tank which can if desired be connected to the mains water supply.

tubes from a main supply pipe.

For smaller pots on staging I like the capillary system of watering. Pot plants are placed on capillary matting which is kept moist. The water enters the pots via the drainage holes and rises up through the compost by capillary action (Fig. 3). The plants take only the amount of water they require and therefore do not become too wet. In most capillary sysems a constant-level water tray, fitted with a valve, is attached to the side of the staging to ensure the correct level of water is maintained.

I would recommend using an automatic watering system only from mid-spring through to early autumn as plants may become too wet in the colder months of the year.

PROPAGATION FACILITIES
The ideal system is to raise plants in a separate greenhouse to take them into the conservatory when they are coming into flower. However, not everybody has a separate greenhouse and it is likely that many people will be raising plants in their conservatory. In any event, wherever you propagate plants, a heated propagating case is strongly recommended for the successful raising of seeds and rooting of cuttings.

There are many to choose from, but for the conservatory I would

Inside view of the Banbury Classic. It provides a spacious and, due to the translucent roof, 'light' extension to the house.

The Banbury Classic conservatory, with its bronze and white finish and translucent fibreglass safety roofing, blends beautifully with many styles of architecture. Size: 4.8 × 3 m (16 × 10 ft).

suggest a propagator that looks attractive, rather than one that is purely utilitarian. Some of the larger, electrically heated propagating cases look like mini-greenhouses, for growing small plants which like very high temperatures and humidity – a form of Wardian case, in fact, which was popular in the Victorian period.

Heating is generally by means of an electrically heated base, the heating elements being sealed in and controlled by a thermostat (Fig. 4).

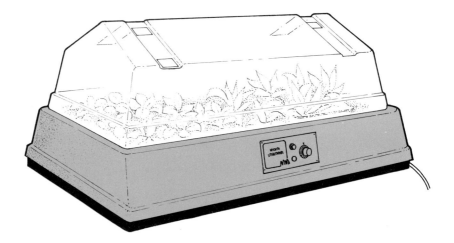

Fig. 4 An electrically heated propagating case is a very useful piece of equipment for the conservatory for it allows one to germinate seeds easily and to root cuttings. Many models are available, generally with heating elements in the base, but try to choose one that is thermostatically controlled so that you can provide the temperature required by the particular subjects. Also, it will be more economical in use.

CONTROL PANELS

To simplify installations in a conservatory there are control panels available, from which you can run, say, lighting, a propagator and an electric heater. These fused control panels are connected to the mains electricity supply. Bear in mind that all electrical installations should be installed by a qualified electrician, and of course all electrical equipment must be of the type specially designed for conservatories and greenhouses – it will be waterproof and therefore completely safe.

CHAPTER 2

PLANNING AND BUILDING

Having decided on the make, style and size of conservatory the next stage is to make sure you have a suitable site for it, to obtain all the necessary planning permission from your local authority and to decide on whether you want to erect it or employ the services of a specialist.

CHOOSING A SITE

Most people will want to build the conservatory against a wall of the house, ideally with access into the house, but one should try to avoid hiding an existing feature.

Do not think that a conservatory can be built only at ground level; some people, who live in town houses, have had elevated conservatories built on first-floor level. They are supported on 'stilts' or pillars.

A conservatory need not be a single-storey structure, either. There are one or two instances of two-storey conservatories, with a staircase joining the upper and lower levels.

There are, of course, no hard and fast rules for siting a conservatory indeed it does not have to be built on the wall of a dwelling house. There are many instances where people have built conservatories against free-standing garden walls, and very good they look, too, very much enhancing the garden.

ASPECT
If possible, though, try to site a conservatory where it receives as much sun as possible. A south-facing wall is best in this respect, or failing that a west-facing wall would be almost as good. If you have no choice but to site the conservatory on a shady wall, such as one facing north or east, then do not despair, for there is a good range of plants that will survive in shady conditions. It will probably be more expensive to heat, though, for you will not be able to rely on the natural warmth of the sun.

Wherever possible try to make sure the site for a conservatory is sheltered from the wind, for cold winds can result in rapid heat loss and this means higher bills. If necessary ensure wind protection by planting

The Banbury California conservatory's elegant flowing lines and attractive antique bronze finish enable it to blend in with many styles of architecture. Due to its shallow roof pitch and low ridge height it is an ideal choice for bungalows, yet there is plenty of headroom. Size: approximately 3.6 × 2.4 m (12 × 8 ft).

a windbreak of, say, conifers, on the windward side, but well away from the conservatory to avoid shade. For instance, one may be able to plant a belt of fast-growing Leyland cypress, × *Cupressocyparis leylandii*. Strong-growing varieties of the Lawson cypress, *Chamaecyparis lawsoniana*, would also make a good windbreak, as would *Thuja plicata*. All of these conifers will form an effective windbreak within a few years.

Try to avoid siting the conservatory where it will be subjected to wind funnelling (Fig. 5). This often occurs in the space between two houses, particularly if they are fairly close together.

You should also try to avoid erecting a conservatory where it will be overshadowed by large trees, for not only will these cast a great amount of shade, but leaves will collect on the roof and in the gutters, and dust and dirt will be washed down from the leaves by rain, creating a lot of grime on the glass. There is also the risk, of course, of falling branches. It is also worth mentioning here that it is a wise precaution to have a wire guard fitted along the eaves of the house roof to prevent tiles or slates from falling onto the conservatory roof.

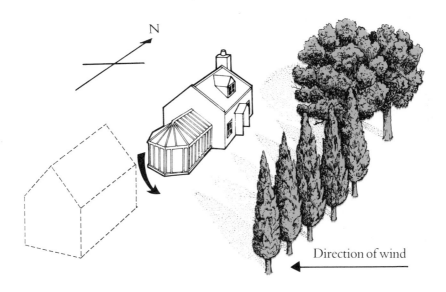

Fig. 5 A conservatory must be carefully sited so that it is not subjected to cold winds, which will result in a great loss of valuable heat. The space between two houses can be a wind tunnel (arrowed) and may need to be avoided. Windbreaks can, perhaps, be planted to filter the wind. Try to avoid shade, e.g. from large trees and, for maximum sun, choose a south-facing wall.

PLANNING PERMISSION AND BUILDING REGULATIONS

Do remember that it is essential to liaise with the planning department of your local authority when you are intending to build a conservatory.

Generally planning permission is not needed for conservatories as they come under permitted development. Permitted development includes extensions of up to 70 m³ (2472 ft³) that are not on any wall fronting onto the highway. Extensions to listed buildings need consent, though. You must check with your local planning department as soon as possible to find out the situation regarding planning permission.

All conservatories on a house need approval under the building regulations, for the base/foundations and the strucure itself must meet with standard specifications.

When you have decided on the make and size of conservatory, and have placed an order, the company will supply a plan and full specifications of the building in order for you to obtain planning permission and approval under the building regulations. At this stage contact your planning department. Many companies supply standard drawings for the base or foundations required.

All of this information must be submitted to your planning department, together with a scale plan of the site (house and garden with the proposed conservatory indicated, too).

If the conservatory is to be built over drains, manhole covers etc, seek advice from any local authority, for building over these must comply with building reguations. For instance, it could well be that manhole and inspection covers may have to be raised and drains reinforced.

The main thing is not to be afraid of the subject of planning permission and building regulations. Most conservatory companies will provide all the advice and information you need to get started, and some can even see the whole procedure through for you. You will also find your local authority very helpful in this respect – after all, it is in their interest to get things right. So do not be afraid to have an initial chat with your planning department, explaining to them exactly what you intend building, and they will then explain to you what you have to do and submit to them.

It is not possible to cover here all the rules and regulations concerning erecting a conservatory, for they do differ slightly from one part of the country to another.

SITE PREPARATION

The conservatory must, of course, be built on an adequate base, complying with building regulations. As a general guide, many conservatories will need a 10 cm (4 in) thick concrete slab laid on at least 10 cm (4 in) of hardcore. The concrete is thickened at the edges to a depth of at least 30 cm (12 in). Then a damp-proof membrane is laid over this followed by a 5 cm deep cement and sand screed (Fig. 6).

Some companies, especially those who supply lean-to greenhouses, provide a pre-fabricated base, which could simply be positioned on concrete footings of a suitable base and your local authority will advise on building regulations.

One has the choice of building the base oneself, or employing a local builder. It is likely that the base, and maybe the completed structure, will be examined by your local building inspector.

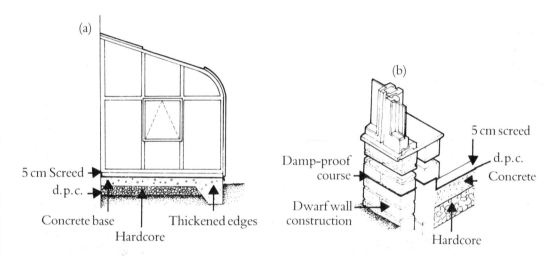

Fig. 6 Conservatories must, of course, be built on substantial bases, complying with building regulations. The usual type of base is the concrete slab with thickened edges (a). Some conservatories, especially modular kinds, are built on dwarf walls, the construction of which is shown in (b); the company supplying the conservatory will provide specifications in this respect.

ERECTING THE CONSERVATORY

Some conservatory companies undertake site erection and glazing, while others may recommend an erection service. A local builder

Another view of the Banbury California, also shown on page 18, which shows how it is enhanced by most attractive landscaping. In this instance, it is used mainly as a living area.

should also be able to erect the conservatory for you, following the manufacturer's instructions.

However, you may prefer to build the conservatory yourself, thereby saving labour costs. Some are easier to assemble than others. For instance, the modular conservatories, which come in sections, are fairly straightforward to put up. More difficult and certainly time-consuming are the metal-framed conservatories and lean-to green-houses. These are supplied in kit form and there are many parts to assemble. However, step-by-step instructions are supplied, and these should be followed to the letter. The different components, e.g. glazing bars, are supplied in separate bundles or packages. I find it a good idea to thoroughly study the erection instructions before making a start, ensuring that I thoroughly understand them. It is certainly advisable to read through the instructions several times before making a start.

Timber-framed lean-to greenhouses and conservatories are easy to erect as they are supplied in sections which are simply bolted together.

From the inside of the house, a view, looking through a living-room window on to the Banbury California conservatory and garden, is a particularly attractive one.

Sometimes the sections are already glazed, but this depends on the manufacturer.

Putting up a conservatory is, of course, much easier if two people are involved, and indeed I would say it is almost essential to have two pairs of hands, especially for the larger structures.

As soon as the conservatory has been erected, do not delay on any timber preservation treatment or painting, as recommended by the manufacturer. If the conservatory is to be painted, it will be delivered with a coat of priming paint, but even so final painting should be completed without delay.

LANDSCAPING THE OUTSIDE

I feel that one should endeavour to blend the conservatory into the garden rather than having a sharp transition between building and garden. This is only a personal view, of course, but nevertheless you might find the following ideas helpful.

BUILDING A PATIO

To my mind the best way to link the conservatory with the rest of the garden is to build a patio around it. There is available today a wide range of pre-cast concrete paving slabs in all shapes, sizes and colour, like natural stone, buff or grey, rather than, say, green or pink. You should try to ensure, though, that the paving harmonizes with the dwelling house and the conservatory.

To be honest, though, there is really nothing to compare with natural-stone, such as York paving. I know this is more expensive than pre-cast concrete slabs but it has a subtle quality that blends with buildings old and new. Concrete paving slabs are more in keeping in a modern setting.

For an old or period property brick paving might be more appropriate and would certainly be a suitable choice for Victorian houses. The paving could perhaps be matched up with the house bricks. There are special hard paving bricks available but do avoid soft bricks, for frost can quickly break them up when laid as a patio. Stock bricks are also used for paving.

Bricks can be laid in various patterns, such as herringbone, or staggered like the bricks in the house walls. Bricks are best loosely laid rather than cementing them down as then they are easily replaced if they become damaged. Lay them flat, rather than on edge, and leave 9 mm (0.35 in) joints which can be filled by brushing sand into them.

CHAPTER 3

LAYING OUT THE INTERIOR

There is a great deal of enjoyment to be derived from choosing a conservatory and seeing it erected, but the most exciting part of all is laying out the interior. Here I am touching on a very personal subject for you will no doubt have your own ideas for floor covering, furnishing and so on. However, I can but put forward ideas, some of which you make like to consider. I have either tried these out myself over the years or have seen them used in other people's conservatories.

Of course, the way in which a conservatory is laid out will depend very much on the way in which you intend using it. A conservatory to be used mainly as a living or working area could well be very different from one used primarily for growing and displaying plants. In the former instance the interior would probably resemble more the rooms in the house, but in the latter case the interior would need to be laid out in a more practical way, with a floor surface that could take water, and the emphasis being on staging and other aids for displaying plants rather than on furnishings

THE FLOOR

This will almost certainly be the first consideration, the floor covering being determined on how you intend using the conservatory. The conservatory, as discussed in Chapter 2, will almost certainly be built on a substantial concrete base, finished off with a smooth cement and sand screed, so this gives an excellent base for ornamental floor coverings.

FLOOR COVERINGS FOR LIVING AREAS

I have often seen pre-cast concrete paving slabs used in conservatories and they can certainly be most attractive. Here the coloured slabs come into their own – they look far better in a conservatory than in the garden. You could perhaps use two different colours, creating a chequer-board effect: say grey and green, or grey and pink. These are best laid on mortar with 6 mm (¼ in) joints which can later be grouted, perhaps with coloured mortar if desired, making sure the grouting is

Some people actually build their own conservatories, which generally means more space for less outlay. This large Victorian-style conservatory, 5.1 × 2.7 m (17 × 9 ft), is a good example, and in fact won for the couple a Homemaker of the Year Competition.

slightly below the level of the slabs. I would suggest you try to obtain non-slip paving slabs: indeed some have a most attractive textured surface.

It is not always a good idea to use the smallest slabs unless you have a very tiny conservatory. For most structures 60 cm (2 ft) square slabs give a more pleasing, less fussy effect.

Quarry tiles look good anywhere and can be used with virtually any style of building. They are often a pleasing heather colour and have a non-slip surface. They are laid in the same way as pre-cast concrete paving slabs but with smaller joints, which are again grouted.

Mats can, of course, be placed on hard surfaces such as concrete paving slabs and quarry tiles – I particularly like rush mats which are available in various sizes and shapes. Mats can also be used on vinyl floor tiles, which are another suitable covering for conservatory floors. There is a wide choice of colours and designs and one can, if desired, lay an attractively patterned floor with these. They are extremely hardwearing and are easily cleaned. Water will not harm them, either. Vinyl tiles are easily laid, using one of the special adhesives available.

As I mentioned above, I am very fond of rush matting in conservatories. This could be used to cover the entire floor, from wall to wall. It can, of course, be laid direct on the smooth cement screed, but first I would suggest treating this with a cement sealant to prevent a dusty surface. Suitable sealents are obtainable from DIY stores, builders' merchants, etc.

Try not to wet the matting, for I find that this results in unsightly marks. Rush matting gives a 'warmer' floor yet is very hardwearing. It is available in various colours, natural as well as shades of brown, etc.

You may prefer to have carpeting in your conservatory and here I would suggest cord carpeting as being the most suitable. It is rather hard on bare feet, but is extremely hardwearing. Again it can be laid on the sealed screed, but in this instance pehaps with a soft underlay. As with rush matting, try not to get this wet – treat it as you would your lounge carpet. As with other kinds of carpeting, there are many colours to choose from.

THE FLOOR IN THE PLANT CONSERVATORY

If the conservatory is to be used for growing plants rather than for living, then you probably need do nothing more than seal the cement screed to prevent a dusty surface. Then you can splash water around to your heart's content. However, if you still want a more attractive floor then lay pre-cast concrete slabs or quarry tiles.

In order to relieve a large expanse of concrete, you could create some gravel areas on which to stand plants, perhaps, or maybe under the staging. The gravel could be contained by small concrete curbing stones, but make sure you leave some small gaps between some of them to allow any excess water to escape. You could use pea shingle for these areas, or one of the horticultural aggregates.

BEDS FOR PLANTING

If you have a reasonably large conservatory you might like to consider constructing soil beds in which to grow plants, an idea much favoured by the Victorians. There is no doubt that plants grow much better in beds than in pots, so much so that shrubs, climbers and other plants could quickly become too large. However, the way to overcome this problem is to choose plants of a suitable size for your conservatory. In my opinion plants look far more natural in soil beds than in pots.

Concerning the construction of soil beds, we have a slight problem if the conservatory is built on a concrete slab – in this case we will have to build raised beds, but this is no bad thing as they can look most attractive.

If the beds are constructed on existing garden soil, the initial

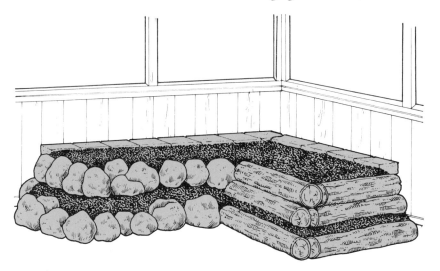

Fig. 7 There is no doubt that plants grow better in soil beds as they have a free root run. If the conservatory is built on a concrete slab then the beds can be raised to provide a most attractive feature. The bed can be tiered or stepped and retaining materials may be natural stone, logs, walling blocks or whatever takes your fancy.

preparation involves digging to two depths of the spade (double digging), breaking up the subsoil well to assist in drainage, and adding bulky organic matter to each trench, such as well-rotted farmyard manure or garden compost.

Beds can be any shape desired – maybe formal, such as a square or rectangular, or informal, of irregular shape. They may be made around the edges of the conservatory or even in the centre if the building is sufficiently large, maybe with paths running through them. There are various materials you could use to construct paths – I like circular pieces of tree trunk, about 7.5 cm (3 in) thick, laid as stepping 'stones'. They are sunk into the soil so that their surfaces are level with the soil surface. Paths can also be made from a coarse grade of pulverized bark, from pea shingle or from one of the horticultural aggregates.

Raised beds are quite easily constructed and they can even be terraced, with several levels rather like wide steps (Fig. 7). Building up can be accomplished with logs or natural stone, or indeed with any material that takes your fancy, such as bricks or ornamental walling blocks.

Do not build beds hard up against the structure, or you will have problems with dampness penetrating the timber. If a bed is to be built near a side of the conservatory it would be better to build a low brick wall at the back, with adequate space between it and the conservatory wall. If the conservatory is built on a low brick wall then you will not have this problem.

You will need a reasonable depth of soil in which to grow plants – about 45 cm (18 in) will be sufficient. Build up the beds with good-quality topsoil, light to medium loam if possible.

If desired, a few well-shaped pieces of rock could be included in the bed, over which low-growing and trailing plants can scramble. The rocks should be partially sunk in the soil.

After planting, the surface of the bed could be mulched with a suitable material to give a pleasing finish. I rather like pulverized bark for mulching, a layer 5–7.5 cm (2–3 in) deep being sufficient. If you are growing cacti in the bed use a layer of coarse sand or gravel.

STAGING FOR POT PLANTS

As mentioned in Chapter 1, staging need not be a permanent fixture and if you buy the type that can be easily dismantled, you can change the layout according to your requirements.

The tiered staging is, of course, designed for positioning against a wall, such as the back wall of the conservatory (Fig. 8). Ordinary

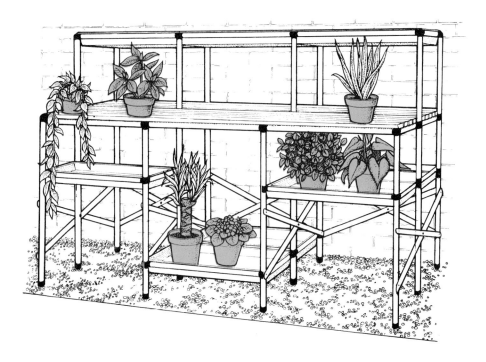

Fig. 8 A very effective way of displaying pot plants is on tiered staging. This allows you to grow more plants in the available space and, of course, makes good use of perhaps otherwise unused vertical space. Tiered staging can be positioned against the back wall of the conservatory. This illustration is of a 'flexible' system – in other words, it can be dismantled and re-assembled in a different formation, and added to, to make it longer or higher. This unit has a combination of slatted timber shelves and plastic capillary watering trays to suit the different requirements of various plants.

staging, the bench type, is generally best arranged around the sides of the conservatory, keeping the centre clear for furniture, etc. However if the conservatory is sufficiently large you may wish to consider having some staging in the centre: perhaps two sets of tiered staging could be used here, placed back to back to give you almost a pyramid-shaped arrangement for displaying plants.

Do not forget that shelving is also available and can be useful for displaying pot plants, especially trailing kinds, on the back wall. There are also special fittings available for putting up shelving in the roof area, again a good way of displaying trailing plants, and also useful in a propagating area for trays of seedlings which need maximum light.

A very handsome, timber-framed, half-octagonal ended conservatory, from Alexander Bartholomew Conservatories Ltd. This is double-glazed and, perhaps because of this, the temperature does not drop below freezing during winter.

Inside view of the same conservatory. Note what an excellent choice cane furniture is for a conservatory as it blends so well with the plants.

SUPPORTS FOR CLIMBING PLANTS

Many plants recommended in Chapter 4 require supports of some kind, for they are climbers. Some of the fruits, too, like grapes and peaches, need supporting. Most plants can be trained to a system of horizontal wires, spaced from 20 to 30 cm (8 to 12 in) apart, on the back wall or even on the sides of the conservatory, and if necessary taken up into the roof area.

Use heavy-gauge galvanized or plastic-coated wire. There are all kinds of fittings available for wires. There are special plugs or fittings available from several companies for securing wires in metal-framed conservatories. For fixing them to timber framework there are metal eye hooks which are screwed into the woodwork. There are wall nails or 'vine eyes' for securing wires to the back wall. All of these ensure the

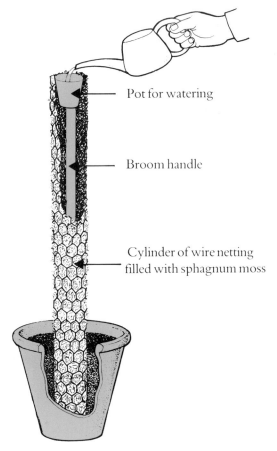

Pot for watering

Broom handle

Cylinder of wire netting filled with sphagnum moss

Fig. 9 A moss pole makes an ideal support for climbing plants of various kinds, especially those which produce aerial roots from their stems, such as the philodendrons and the Swiss cheese plant or *Monstera deliciosa*. The roots grow into the moss, which should be kept moist at all times by pouring water into the pot at the top. This is a home-made version, consisting of a broom handle surrounded by moss, which is held in place with a cylinder of wire netting.

wires are an inch or two from the wall, to allow for air circulation behind the plants. Plants are tied in with soft garden string or raffia.

Ornamental plants could also be trained to trellis work fixed to a wall. There is a wide range of trellis panels available in various shapes and sizes. You may opt for wooden trellis, or the more modern plastic-coated steel trellis. Suitable fittings or brackets are available to secure the panels an inch or two from the wall.

There are even small trellis panels available for plants growing in pots; and also for pot work, ordinary bamboo canes make good supports for small climbing plants.

Many plants, such as some of the philodendrons, can be grown up moss poles. These are ideal for those plants which produce aerial roots, for these grow into the moss and help to support the plant.

A moss pole can be used in a pot or in a soil bed and is very easily made (Fig. 9). Use a broom handle of suitable length and insert this well into the soil. Place over this a cylinder of small-mesh wire netting, extending it below the soil surface. Then pack the cylinder with live sphagnum moss, which you should be able to obtain from a florist. A small pot can be inserted in the top of the wire cyclinder and rested on the top of the broom handle. This provides an easy means of keeping the moss moist – simply pour water into the pot and it will trickle down through the moss. If you do not use this method, keep the moss moist be spraying it as necessary with a hand sprayer. If you want to make a taller and thicker moss column, then use a wooden fencing post or tree stake. This would provide a more adequate support for larger plants.

A PLANT TREE FOR EPIPHYTES

In the lists in Chapter 4 you will see that some plants are epiphytic, especially many of the bromeliads. This means that in the wild they grow on trees (or occasionally on rocks). Many epiphytes will grow well enough in pots, but they look more natural if grown on a dead tree or a piece of branch. The air plants or atmospheric tillandsias will not grow in pots and have to be mounted on wood of some kind.

In any case, a tree bearing a collection of bromeliads and other epiphytic plants makes a stunning feature in the conservatory (Fig. 10). The idea comes from the USA where this method of growing is popular. It is gradually catching on in other countries as people come to realize how attractive a plant tree can be. Some garden centres are leading the way and are now displaying plants in this way and examples can also be seen in botanic gardens.

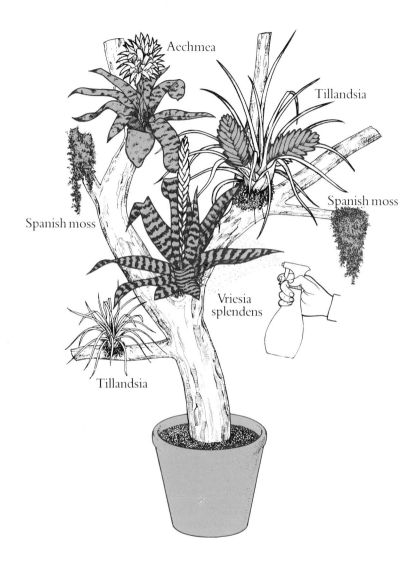

Aechmea

Tillandsia

Spanish moss

Spanish moss

Vriesia
splendens

Tillandsia

Fig. 10 The best way to grow epiphytic or tree-dwelling plants, like many of the bromeliads (some of which are shown here), is on a plant tree. The plants can be tied onto the tree, or planted in little pockets formed from a piece of bark nailed to the tree. Watering is accomplished by spraying the plants and the tree with water. A plant tree is made from a section of tree or from a suitably branched tree branch. It can, of course, be any size desired, and in this illustration it has been cemented into a clay flower pot.

The tree can, of course, be any height required, from perhaps 1 m (3 ft) to almost the height of the conservatory roof. The tree should be dead but perfectly sound – in other words, not starting to rot. I use the term tree, but generally one would use a tree branch, ideally one that is well-branched. But where does one obtain a tree branch? On no account chop off a tree in the the countryside. You may be permitted to take a fallen tree branch but you must seek permission first. Or there may be some tree pruning or felling going on in your locality – perhaps in a park or neighbour's garden. Ask if you can have a branch.

The tree should be inserted firmly in a soil bed, reasonably deeply, ramming the soil all around it. If you do not have a soil bed, use a pot of suitable size. The tree is positioned in the centre and the pot filled with mortar. Do not use soil or the tree will not be sufficiently firm.

There are various ways of securing plants to a tree. You could fix small specimens to separate pieces of bark before setting them on the tree, as this will allow you to move them around if desired. Large, heavier plants, however, are best fixed directly on the tree. Maybe you can wedge them in the crotches of branches, or make small planting pockets with pieces of bark or cork bark nailed to the tree. These can be filled with suitable compost.

If plants are supplied in pots, remove them and tease away some of the compost before securing them to the tree. Surround the roots with sphagnum moss to hold the compost in place.

On no account place compost or moss around the roots of the air plants or atmospheric tillandsias (if indeed they have any roots) or the plants will rot.

The plants can be secured to the tree or to pieces of bark with a thin nylon string or with copper wire or plastic-coated wire. Do not tie them on too tightly, though, or the tying material may cut into the plants. Such tying materials can also be used to hold in sphagnum moss around the roots.

The plants are watered by spraying the entire tree with water. I think you will find that epiphytic plants grow much better on a tree and they are certainly easier to maintain.

HANGING CONTAINERS

A good way of displaying trailing or pendulous plants is in hanging containers, perhaps fixed in the roof of the conservatory. However, there are available all kinds of ornamental brackets which can be used to support hanging containers on the walls. I particularly like black wrought-iron brackets for this purpose.

There are several kinds of hanging container, the best-known traditional galvanized-wire type (or plastic-coated in more modern versions) and the moulded plastic type. Often the latter have a built-in drip tray. Wire baskets are lined with sphagnum moss before planting. I would suggest that the moulded plastic baskets are more suitable for the 'lived-in' conservatory as there is no risk of drips when watering.

There are other kinds of hanging container including pots, in terracotta, ceramic or plastic.

Pots of trailing plants can also be displayed on wall trellis. There are available special brackets which support pot holders and these are designed for the modern plastic-coated steel trellis. Not enough use is made of walls for displaying pot plants – the idea is more popular in USA, yet it can be most effective.

HEATING THE CONSERVATORY

I have discussed temperatures in Chapter 5 so here I will consider the various methods of heating a conservatory.

Wherever possible I would suggest running the domestic heating system into the conservatory as this would surely provide the most economical means of heating. However, this would not be suitable for a conservatory devoted only to plants, where there may be a lot of moisture.

If it is not possible to run in a domestic system then an independent heating system will have have to be considered. One has a choice of gas or electric heaters, paraffin heaters or a boiler system with hot-water pipes. There are many companies who supply heaters specially designed for greenhouses and conservatories. I would emphasize it is best to use a heater designed for horticultural use, especially if there is a lot of moisture in the conservatory.

ELECTRIC HEATERS
Electricity is an excellent choice for it is clean, efficient, reliable, automatic and generally convenient. Electricity gives off dry heat so a dry atmosphere will be created.

However it is a very expensive fuel, as we all know, but heaters have thermostatic control for economical running. Remember you should employ a qualified electrician to install the electricity supply.

Fan heaters are one type of electric greenhouse heater. These consist of a small portable cabinet with a fan and heating element, and warm air is blown out. They have the advantage of keeping the air moving. Do not allow a fan heater to blow directly onto plants.

Tubular heaters consist of hollow tubes, inside of which are heating elements. They are generally installed in banks along the sides of the conservatory. I consider they are very neat and compact.

Convection heaters are basically cabinets with heating elements inside to warm the air. As the warm air rises out of the top of the cabinet, so cool air is drawn in at the bottom. Like fan heaters, the convection type keeps the air moving. Convection heaters are particularly recommended for large conservatories.

GAS HEATERS

Gas heaters are very popular for heating conservatories and green-houses. If you have a supply of natural gas, then buy a natural-gas type of heater. This would be cheaper to run than bottled gas. A gas heater is basically a warm–air cabinet and is thermostatically controlled. Gas gives off carbon dioxide, which is beneficial to plants, and also gives off water vapour which will prevent the atmosphere from becoming too dry. You will need to employ a professional gas engineer to install the gas supply and connect up the heater.

Heaters which run off bottled gas are similar but they are portable. Again one has thermostatic control. They run off propane or butane gas and need the minimum of attention and maintenance. You will find that buying large gas cylinders rather than small ones is more economical.

PARAFFIN HEATERS

I am not altogether convinced that paraffin heaters are the best means of heating a conservatory, although they are cerainly more efficient than they used to be. Most are really only adequate for keeping a conservatory frost free, not for maintaining high temperatures, and therefore are perhaps better suited to normal greenhouses, where they are widely used.

Themostatic control is available on some models. There are two basic types: the blue–flame heater, with less risk of fumes being produced, and the yellow–flame heater, which is almost as good as the former. Advantages are that paraffin heaters are comparatively cheap to buy and run, are portable, and give off carbon dioxide, which is appreciated by plants.

There are several disadvantages though: they need frequent attention; a lot of water vapour is produced, resulting in condensation; some ventilation must be given at all times; and they can give off harmful fumes (harmful to plants) if not regularly cleaned.

Some models can be fitted with pipes or ducts to distribute the heat more efficiently. Always use high-grade paraffin and avoid placing the heater in a draught.

BOILER SYSTEMS

A boiler and hot-water pipes is, of course, an old-fashioned method of heating, but modern systems are very efficient and need minimum attention. Such a system is ideal for a large conservatory and where high temperatures are required. The boiler, which must be under cover outside the conservatory, can be fired by solid fuel, oil or mains gas. Solid fuel is recommended if you want to maintain high temperatures with realistic running costs. You have automation, of course, if you opt for oil or gas. Minimum attention is needed, however, even with solid fuel. Hot-water pipes, which run around the walls, give out dry heat.

There are one or two disadvantages: a boiler system does not respond very quickly to temperature changes, it is rather bulky, and there will be daily stoking and ash clearing if solid fuel is used. The suppliers will advise on size of boiler and necessary pipe length for your conservatory, according to the temperature you wish to maintain.

SIZE OF HEATER REQUIRED

The heat output must be sufficient to maintain the temperature you require in your size of conservatory. You will find that most heater manufacturers/suppliers will advise on this, if you state the size of your conservatory and the temperature range you wish to maintain. Generally, a heater should have a slightly higher output than needed, to be sure that it can cope in periods of really severe weather.

LIGHTING

Obviously some form of lighting will be needed and can be provided by means of fluorescent tubes fitted in the roof area.

There are also various kinds of decorative lighting available these days, designed for use in conservatories. For instance, one can illuminate an ornamental plant display at night. Spot lights can be used, perhaps to highlight plants which have especially attractive leaves, or which have a spectacular flower display.

You must make sure that lighting systems are specially designed for conservatory use, and have them installed by a qualified electrician.

DECORATING THE BACK WALL

I think it is often a good idea to paint the back wall of the conservatory a light colour to help reflect light, especially if it is brickwork. If it is rendered then the normal practice anyway is to paint the entire house walls.

If the house walls are already painted, you will probably want to use the same colour inside the conservatory. If not, then I would suggest you use white or cream, whichever matches up best with the framework of the conservatory. Use a good-quality masonry paint: the modern ones which contain fine sand are very long lasting and some of them give a textured finish.

An inside view of a custom-made conservatory. This one is south facing and, as can be seen, a grape vine, trained up into the roof, flourishes here.

CHAPTER 4

PLANTS FOR ALL SEASONS

There is a wealth of plants available for growing in the conservatory, from those which can take very cool conditions to flamboyant tropical kinds. Of course, they should be chosen to suit the minimum temperature you are able to maintain; but whatever this minimum may be, you can be assured there are sufficient plants to provide colour and interest all the year round.

Many people will not be able to provide sufficient heat to keep tropical plants flourishing during the autumn winter and early spring. Nevertheless, such plants can be displayed in the conservatory during the warmer summer months, and indeed they will greatly benefit from a spell under glass. For the rest of the year they can be kept in a warm room indoors and treated as houseplants.

The following descriptive lists contain some of the most popular plants for growing in conservatories. The shrubs and climbers will provide a permanent 'framework' to the planting scheme, especially if planted in beds and borders, corms and tubers.

To my mind, plenty of foliage plants should be used, too, to provide a lush 'jungle' atmosphere, and to act as a foil to brightly coloured flowers. There is great diversity in leaf shape (from sword-like to hand-shaped leaves), colour and texture, as a glance at the foliage-plant list will show.

And finally do not forget fruits: I have included the traditional conservatory kinds: grapes, peaches and nectarines.

TEMPERATURES

The lists contain all the basic cultural information you are likely to need. Do bear in mind that the temperature quoted for each plant is the *minimum* acceptable temperature. Most plants will enjoy higher temperatures than these by day and during the summer.

SHRUBS

ABUTILON
Temperature: 10° C (50° F).

Characteristics: The abutilons are easily grown shrubs and some of the taller-growing kinds are amenable to training on walls, pillars, etc. Most are grown for their attractive bell-shaped flowers produced in summer, but do consider also those with coloured variegated foliage. Most have fairly large leaves, rather maple-like in shape. For flowers I can recommend several of the hybrids, particularly 'Ashford Red', which is crimson; the beautiful yellow 'Canary Bird' or 'Golden Fleece'; and the red-orange 'Firebell'. For variegated foliage, one of the most striking is the hybrid 'Savitzii', with white and green leaves. Unlike the other hybrids, which grow up to 1.8 m (6 ft), this one is a low grower and makes a fine pot specimen. Tall, and suitable for training, is *A. striatum* 'Thompsonii' which has striking yellow-mottled leaves.

Cultivation: Any well-drained soil is suitable, and if pot grown I prefer to use soil-based compost. Water and feed plants well in summer and provide an airy atmosphere. To prevent leggy growth plants are best pruned hard back in early spring each year. Easily propagated from cuttings in summer.

ACACIA Wattle

Temperature: 10° C (50° F), or slightly lower.

Characteristics: The wattles are evergreen shrubs or trees, many of them quite tall. The foliage is attractive and masses of small, powder-puff-like flowers appear in spring. Most easily available are the Cootamunda wattle, *A. baileyana*, with bluish-grey foliage, and the silver wattle, *A. dealbata*, with silvery foliage (this is the one you see in florists' shops).

Cultivation: Good drainage is needed, plus maximum light and plenty of ventilation (in winter as well if the weather is mild). Water well in summer but keep only slightly moist in winter. Routine pruning is not required but as the plants grow tall you will need to cut them back when they reach the roof and this is best done immediately flowering is over. I find wattles are best grown against a wall of the conservatory to prevent them spreading too much.

BRUNFELSIA

Temperature: 10° C (50° F).

Characteristics: These are spectacular but easy evergreen shrubs which are suited to the small conservatory and they bloom over a long period in the summer. The best-known species is *B. calycina* with scented, fairly large blue-purple flowers. There are several varieties of this which are well worth searching for, including *B.c. floribunda* which

This tall L-shaped conservatory extends to the first-floor level of the house. Note the attractive cast-iron staircase which blends beautifully with the timber construction and aluminium glazing bars for the roof.

has darker flowers, and *B.c. macrantha* which is noted for its larger blooms. I am also particularly fond of the species *B. latifolia* with scented blooms of a pale violet shade, and *B. undulata* which has fragrant white blooms, attractively waved at the edges.

Cultivation: Best grown in a soil bed, but happy in a large pot or tub in well-drained soil-based compost. I pinch out the growing tips of young plants to ensure bushy, well-branched specimens. General cultivation is simple enough: shade from strong sun, water as required in the growing season, plus occasional liquid feeds, with less water in autumn and winter. Established plants do not need pruning.

CALLISTEMON Bottle brush
Temperature: 4.5° C (40° F).
Characteristics: Ideal shrubs for the small cool conservatory, producing in summer unusual flowers, which do indeed look like a bottle brush. They are Australian shrubs, with evergreen foliage, and the blooms are generally in shades of red. The flowers consist mainly of long stamens and it is these which form the 'brush'. Buy whichever species you find on offer: it could be *C. citrinus. C. linearis, C. rigidus, C. speciosus* or *C. subulatus.* Each one is well worth growing.

Cultivation: Callistemons can be grown in a soil bed or in pots, and drainage must be very good, soil-based compost being recommended for pot culture. Soil or compost must be acid or lime-free.

As with most Australian shrubs, provide plenty of ventilation and ensure plants receive a good quantity of sunshine. If plants are pot grown, stand them out of doors for the summer in a sunny sheltered spot. This will help to ripen the new shoots.

CAMELLIA
Temperature: 4.5–10° C (40–50° F); also unheated conservatory.
Characteristics: These evergreen shrubs have shiny dark green foliage which makes a superb background for the red, pink or white flowers which are produced in winter or spring. Camellias are hardy and can also be grown out of doors. I recommend cultivars of *C. japonica*, and there are many hundreds to choose from. Garden centres stock a limited range, but if you want a wider choice buy from a camellia specialist. Also try some of the *C. reticulata* and *C. × williamsii* cultivars: highly popular is *C. × williamsii* 'Donation' with large, semi-double orchid-pink flowers.

Cultivation: I think in the amateur conservatory plants are best grown in pots, potting them on until eventually they are in tubs. It is essential to use an acid or lime-free compost. I make up a mix consisting of mainly peat and leafmould, but add a little coarse sand and acid loam. If you do not want to go to this trouble, buy a proprietary ericaceous compost from a garden centre. The plants are taken under glass in the autumn; provide really good ventilation and make sure the compost does not dry out. It should be kept steadily moist but not wet.

When flowering is over stand the plants outside in a sheltered, semi-shaded spot. Ideally plunge the pots in weathered ashes so that the compost does not dry out rapidly. Keep the compost steadily moist throughout the growing season. In the summer plants will benefit from liquid feeding every two weeks. Try to use rainwater for watering if you have 'hard' tapwater.

CESTRUM
Temperature: 7–10° C (45–50° F).
Characteristics: These are fairly tall evergreen or semi-evergreen shrubs but nevertheless are suitable for the smallish conservatory if they are grown against a wall or pillar to stop the stems from spreading outwards. They are grown for their clusters of tubular flowers which appear in summer and autumn. There are several species which are fairly easily obtainable, including the bright orange C. *aurantiacum*, 3 m (10 ft); the red-purple C. *elegans*, 3 m; the crimson C. 'Newellii', 2 m (6 ft); and the bright pink C. *roseum*, also 2 m.
Cultivation: Grow in a soil bed if possible, or failing that a large tub. The growing medium should be high in humus so add plenty of peat to the soil or use a peat-based potting compost. The plants will take plenty of water in the growing season, but ease up in autumn and winter. Feed regularly in summer and provide shade from strong sun. Train the stems to a system of horizontal wires, and allow if desired the stems to grow into the roof area. In late winter carry out pruning: remove all three-year-old stems, and prune out the old flowered tops of those remaining.

DATURA Angel's trumpets
Temperature: 10° C (50° F), or slightly lower.
Characteristics: Large, vigorous, evergreen or deciduous shrubs with huge trumpet-shaped blooms in the summer and autumn – hence the common name. They are more suitable for the larger conservatory. Serval species which you may come across in garden centres include D. *cornigera* with scented white or cream flowers, 3 m (10 ft); D.c. 'Knightii', a double-flowered form in the same colour; the superb orange-red D. *sanguinea*, 2 m (6 ft); and the well-scented white D. *suaveolens*, a giant at 5 m (16 ft).

Cultivation: Daturas are best grown in a soil border due to their vigour, but I have had good results with large pots. In summer a good deal of ventilation should be provided with light shade from strong sunshine. Despite the fact they are vigorous, the plants benefit from regular feeding during the summer about once a fortnight, with liquid fertilizer. To restrict the height of these shrubs, cut back last year's stems to within 15 cm (6 in) of ground level in late winter.

ERYTHRINA Coral tree

Temperature: 4.5° C (40° F).

Characteristics: This is one of my great favourites for it has flamboyant flowers in summer, and despite the fact that it is a native of Brazil, it is almost hardy and easily grown. The species grown is *E. crista-galli* (the specific name meaning cock's comb), which produces scarlet pea-like flowers. The leaves are trifoliate and carried on spiny stems which grow to about 2 m (6 ft) in height.

Cultivation: In the spring and summer make sure the plant has really good light and ventilation. Water as required in the growing season, but in winter the soil or compost should be kept virtually dry as the plant will be resting. The leaves fall in autumn. In spring cut back all stems to within a few centimetres of soil. New stems will then be produced. Grow in a large pot or tub, or in a soil border. Drainage must be good. I raised my plants from seeds sown in heat in spring and they made terrific growth during the first season.

HIBISCUS Shrubby mallow

Temperature: 10° C (50° F).

Characteristics: The species usually grown is *H. rosa-sinensis,* which is a very common sight in hotel gardens in the Mediterranean countries. The plant originates from China, though. It is a deciduous shrub with large flared deep-red flowers in summer. Height is about 2 m (6 ft). In recent years many cultivars have come on the market whose colours include red, pink, yellow, orange and white. An old culivar is *H. rosa-sinensis* 'Cooperi' whose leaves are variegated white and green. The flowers are red.

Cultivation: I prefer to grow hibiscus in a soil bed, but good results are possible in large pots or tubs. Use a well-drained soil-based compost when potting. Only light shade from strong sun is needed in summer, but high humidity is desirable. Water well in summer, and feed regularly, but keep only slightly moist in winter. In late winter plants can be pruned fairly hard to keep them small.

LANTANA
Temperature: 7° C (45° F).

Characteristics: *Lantana camara* is a small shrub from the West Indies and has become naturalized throughout the tropics. It's ideal for the small conservatory, bearing a long succession of yellow flowers in summer and autumn. There are several cultivars which may have yellow, pink, red or white blooms.

Cultivation: If grown in a soil bed it will make quite a wide-spreading bush, but it is also suitable for pot cultivation. Ensure well-drained soil or compost. A good deal of sunshine is needed plus plenty of ventilation in the summer. Keep only slightly moist during the autumn and winter. I prefer to replace plants frequently with young specimens, which are more compact. Cuttings taken in spring or early summer are easily rooted in a heated propagating case. Pinch out the tips of young plants to create bushy specimens. In early spring older plants can be cut back to within 15 cm (6 in) of compost level. This prevents plants becoming leggy, straggly and bare of foliage at the base.

NERIUM Oleander
Temperature: 7° C (45° F).

Characteristics: *Nerium oleander* is a familiar sight in Mediterranean gardens, from where it originates. It is an evergreen shrub to about 2 m (6 ft) in height and in summer and autumn bears pink, red, or purple-red blooms. Look out, too, for cultivars, such as the double white 'Album Plenum', the double pink 'Roseum Plenum', and 'Variegatum', whose leaves are edged with cream.

Cultivation: Basic conditions to provide are good ventilation and plenty of sun. I find that plants benefit from a spell out of doors in the summer, taking them inside again during early autumn. Carry out watering as necessary in the spring and summer, but in autumn and winter keep the soil or compost on the dry side. Apply liquid fertilizer fortnightly in summer. I prefer to grow plants in pots, eventually moving them to large pots or tubs. Use soil-based compost for best results, as drainage is better than with peat-based types and oleanders certainly need good drainage.

RHODODENDRON
Temperature: 7° C (45° F)

Characteristics: The tender rhododendrons are ideal subjects for the cool conservatory. The most popular is the so-called Indian azalea, cultivars of *R. simsii*, which bloom in the autumn and winter. At that period garden centres and florists' shops are full of these azaleas, which

Foliage plants provide a good foil and background for flowering pot plants such as thunbergia (yellow flowers), blue streptocarpus and busy Lizzie or impatiens (red flowers).

come in various colours – shades of pink, red, white, etc. Cultivars of the similar *R. indicum* are also available. Both types are low-growing evergreens. More difficult to obtain are several other tender rho-dodendrons, such as *R. lindleyi* with highly fragrant white waxy blooms. This is a large shrub, growing to about 3 m (10 ft) in height.
Cultivation: Soil or compost for rhododendrons must be acid or lime-free. They can be grown in a soil bed, but are more generally pot grown. Use an ericaceous compost, or mix your own: equal parts by volume of peat and leafmould, plus some coarse sand and a little fertilizer. Water regularly throughout the year as the soil or compost must not be allowed to dry out. In summer apply liquid fertilizer once a fortnight, plenty of ventilation, moderate humidity, and light shade from strong sun. I place the Indian azaleas out of doors for the summer, in a sheltered spot with dappled shade, such as under a tree.

TIBOUCHINA Glory bush
Temperature: 10° C (50° F).
Characteristics: *Tibouchina semidecandra,* the species generally grown, is an evergreen shrub from Brazil, attaining about 3 m (10 ft) in height. It has attractive velvety leaves, and in summer and autumn produces beautiful blue-purple, saucer-shaped blooms.
Cultivation: Grow in a soil border or in pots of soil-based potting compost. Water normally in spring and summer, but keep only just moist in winter. If you do not wish to restrict size, tibouchina makes a good wall shrub – train it up the back wall of the conservatory and even up into the roof. Pot-grown plants will need to have their stems supported with thin bamboo canes.

CLIMBERS

BOUGAINVILLEA Paper flower
Temperature: 10° C (50° F).
Characteristics: This vigorous Brazilian climber is a popular con-servatory plants and despite its flamboyant appearance is easily grown. The flowers are insignificant: it is the highly colourful paper-like bracts that surround them which create the display in summer. Two species are generally available: *B. glabra,* widely planted in the Mediterranean countries, with purple bracts, and *B. spectabilis,* with reddish or purple bracts. In recent years many named hybrids have become available like the orange 'Golden Glow'; 'Mrs Butt', crimson to magenta; 'Brilliant', copper-orange and 'Orange King', with orange bracts.

Cultivation: Ideal for large-pot cultivation, using a well-drained soil-based compost, or for a soil bed. If you do not have much space grow in a pot and train it to a framework of canes – the stems can be looped to keep them within bounds. Carry out regular pruning in early spring by removing all weak or spindly shoots. The strong remaining stems can then be cut back by at least one-third if necessary. Bougainvilleas need plenty of sunshine, good ventilation and high humidity in summer. In winter, keep soil/compost on the dry side and increase watering as growth commences in the spring.

CLIANTHUS Parrot's bill
Temperature: 7–10° C (45–50° F).
Characteristics: These climbers, which are in the pea family, come from Australia and New Zealand and are ideal for the cool conservatory. The pinnate foliage is attractive and the large pea-like blooms in spring or summer will be the envy of your visitors. *C. puniceus* is the species usually grown. It attains a modest 2 m (6 ft) in height and has red flowers. There is also a white form of this called 'Albus'.
Cultivation: Grow the parrot's bill in a border or large pot, ensuring drainage is very good. Use a soil-based compost for pot culture and put plenty of drainage material in the bottom. Very good light is needed but a little shade from the strongest sun will be appreciated. Water normally when in full growth but be sparing in winter.

HOYA Wax flower
Temperature: 7° C (45° F).
Characteristics: *Hoya carnosa,* a native of Queensland, is one of the most popular climbers for the conservatory and ideally suited to the smaller structure. It is evergreen, having rather thick fleshy leaves, and is rather a slow grower. Pendulous clusters of white waxy flowers, which turn pinkish as they age, are produced in the summer.
Cultivation: Best grown in a soil bed well supplied with peat, as a humus-rich soil is enjoyed. Can be pot grown, though, in which case you should use a proprietary peat-based potting compost. When pot grown the stems can be twined around a system of canes or wire hoops. In summer give light shade and maintain a humid atmosphere. Water normally, but in autumn and winter allow the soil or compost to almost dry out before applying water. Feed fortnightly in summer with a liquid fertilizer. Good light is needed in winter. No pruning is necessary. If plants are cut back they are slow to recover, so if a plant becomes too large it is better to replace it with a young specimen.

JASMINUM Jasmine

Temperature: 4.5° C (40° F).

Characteristics: The jasmines create a heady atmosphere in the conservatory during the spring or summer with their deliciously fragrant flowers. The most easily obtainable species is the white-flowered *J. polyanthum*. Very attractive, though, are the yellow-flowered *J. primulinum* and *J. mesnyi,* so these are well worth looking out for.

Cultivation: The jasmines are easy to grow and do well in a soil bed or in pots. In summer they like an airy atmosphere and light shade from strong sunshine. Water as required throughout the year. You may need to prune in late winter if growth becomes congested or if you wish to contain the plant. Thin out older growth and leave as much young wood as possible which will produce flowers. Reduce the height if necessary but do not be too severe with the secateurs.

LAPAGERIA Chilean bellflower

Temperature: 4.5–7° C (40–45° F).

Characteristics: *Lapageria rosea,* from Chile, must be the most popular climber of all time. It is evergreen and attains a height of about 3 m (10 ft). In the late summer and autumn it produces large, tubular, waxy blooms in a beautiful shade of crimson. There is a white variety available but this is less popular.

Cultivation: Best grown in a soil bed but also suitable for large pots. Acid or lime-free soil or compost is needed, and if pot grown use a proprietary acid peat-based compost. Mix plenty of peat or leafmould into a soil bed before planting. Cultivation is straightforward: good ventilation and light shade in summer, normal watering all year round, and no pruning.

PASSIFLORA Passion flower

Temperature: 10° C (50° F).

Characteristics: These vigorous climbers are easy to grow and ideal for the cool conservatory. They flower in the summer and have the most intricate floral structure. The best known is the common blue Passion flower, *P. caerulea*, but others I can recommend include *P.* × *caeruleo-racemosa* with purple blooms; the deep pink *P.* × *exoniensis;* and the pink or light violet *P. quadrangularis*.

Cultivation: Ideally grow in a soil bed, but plants can be grown in pots of soil-based compost. In summer the plants like a humid atmosphere and light shade, together with ample watering. In autumn and winter water very sparingly: only when the soil/compost is starting to dry out. I would not recommend feeding as the plants are naturally very vigorous. Pruning can be carried out in late winter: when the plants become congested, thin out the oldest stems and leave the younger ones. The side shoots on the stems remaining can be cut back to within 15 cm (6 in) of their base. If you have only a small conservatory you may find that the Passion flowers are a bit too large.

PLUMBAGO
Temperature: 7° C (45° F).
Characteristics: The South African *Plumbago capensis* is an ideal climber for the small cool conservatory, attaining about 3 m (10 ft) in height. A succession of blue flowers is produced in summer and autumn. Also attractive is the white variety 'Alba'.
Cultivation: Grow in a soil bed or pot, using well-drained soil-based compost. Lightly shade from strong sunshine in summer, feed once a fortnight and water regularly. Keep the soil/compost only slighly moist during the autumn and winter. In late winter carry out pruning: cut back the side shoots to within a few centimetres of their base and shorten the main stems by about one-third.

FLOWERING POT PLANTS

SHORT-TERM PLANTS
Most of these plants are raised annually from seeds and provide colour at various times of the year. They are discarded after flowering.

ANNUALS, HARDY
Temperature: Best in a very cool conservatory, which is just frost free: do not subject plants to high temperatures.
Characteristics: Various hardy annuals make excellent pot plants for flowering in spring, such as clarkia, cornflower *(Centaurea cyanus)*, *Echium plantagineum*, godetia, and *Lavatera trimestris*. Also try these biennials: Canterbury bells *(Campanula medium)*, and foxgloves or digitalis.
Cultivation: Sow the seeds in late summer, but late spring for Canterbury bells and foxgloves. Germinate the seeds in a cold frame and prick off seedlings into 9 cm (3½ in) pots. Use well-drained soil-based potting compost. Grow on the young plants in a cold frame with plenty of ventilation. Canterbury bells and foxgloves are best grown out of doors and put into a cold frame in early autumn.

Pot on young plants in early to mid-autumn, using 12.5 cm (5 in) pots. Final potting into 15 cm (6 in) pots should be completed by late autumn. The plants are moved into the conservatory in early winter.

Do make sure the conservatory is well ventilated, and water the plants very carefully. The compost should be kept only slightly moist: if too wet the plants may rot off. When the plants start growing more rapidly in spring increase watering and feed with a liquid fertilizer about once a fortnight. Taller plants will need to be supported with canes and soft string.

CALCEOLARIA Slipper wort
Temperature: 7° C (45° F).

Characteristics: These are popular plants, producing large pouched flowers in brilliant colours during spring or early summer. Seedsmen offer many mixed strains, with flower in shades of red, yellow, orange etc. often attractively spotted.

Cultivation: Sow the seeds in early summer and as they are very small do not cover them with compost. Germinate them in a cold frame. The seedlings are pricked off into seed trays and before they become overcrowded are potted into 7.5 cm (3 in) pots. Grow on in a cold frame with plenty of ventilation. The frame lights can be taken off when the weather is fine. In autumn pot into 12.5 cm (5 in) pots and move the plants into the conservatory. It is essential to keep calceolaries cool at all times and they will not need more than 7° C in the winter. Ventilate well and keep the compost steadily moist in winter but avoid very wet compost. Pot on the plants into final 15 cm (6 in) pots in late winter. Calceolarias can be grown equally well in soil-based or peat-based compost.

CAPSICUM Ornamental pepper
Temperature: 10° C (50° F).

Characteristics: Capsicums are grown for their ornamental fruits which are produced in the autumn and winter. Generally the fruits are cone-shaped but may be round in some varieties. They come in shades of red, yellow and orange. The varieties offered by seedsmen are dwarf plants and hybrids of *C. annuum* and *C. frutescens*. Some popular varieties include 'Holiday Time', 'Fips', 'Holiday Cheer' and 'Inferno'.

Cultivation: Sow the seeds in mid-spring and germinate in a heated propagating case. Prick out the seedlings into 7.5 cm (3 in) pots. Before they become pot-bound move on into final 12.5 cm (5 in) pots. Soil-based or peat-based composts are suitable. Provide good ventilation and shade from the sun. When the plants are in flower I spray them overhead with plain water each day to ensure good pollination and consequently a good 'set' of berries.

CELOSIA Prince of Wales' feathers
Temperature: 10° C (50° F)
Characteristics: I am a great admirer of *Celosia plumosa* with its feathery flower heads in the summer in shades of red, yellow, apricot and pink. Many strains are offered by seedsmen, including 'Kewpie Red', 'Kewpie Yellow', 'Geisha Mixed', 'Fairy Fountains' and the superb 'Apricot Brandy' with apricot-orange plumes. They are dwarf pot plants, averaging 30 cm (12 in) in height.
Cultivation: Seeds are sown in early or mid-spring and should be germinated in a heated propagating case. Prick out the seedlings individually into 7.5 cm (3 in) pots and before they become pot bound pot into final 12.5 cm (5 in) pots. Use soil-based or well-drained peat-based compost. Celosias like good light but will need shade from the strongest sun. Regular feeding in summer ensures really strong plants. Water normally but do not allow the compost to become saturated.

CHRYSANTHEMUM
Temperature: Cool or unheated conservatory.
Characteristics: Greenhouse chrysanthemums rank among the most important plants for autumn colour in the conservatory. The various types available and their cultivation constitute a very big subject and indeed there are many boo's devoted to chrysanthemums. Suffice to say here that there are large-flowered chrysanthemums like the greenhouse decoratives, single-flowered kinds like large daisies, and small-flowered spray and anemone-centred kinds. When making a choice of varieties it is best to consult a catalogue from a specialist chysanthemum grower.
Cultivation: Plants are pot-grown, using soil-based compost. Early in the year rooted cuttings are potted into small pots, and are gradually potted on until they are in final 20 cm (8 in) pots. I always use soil-based compost. Young plants are grown on in a cold frame from early spring onwards, and from early summer onwards are grown out of doors.

The young plants should be stopped or pinched out when about 15 cm (6 in) high. Plenty of water and feeding is needed in summer, and in early autumn the plants are arranged in the conservatory to flower, when plenty of ventilation must be given to keep the air dry. The old flowered plants are cut down and kept over the winter in a cold frame to give cuttings in the following early spring.

I think the charm chrysanthemums are superb conservatory plants. They make bushy specimens about 45 cm (18 in) in height and cover

In the cool conservatory summer foliage colour can be provided by coleus, which will develop into very large specimens if regularly potted on. Here, further colour is provided by purple streptocarpus and the trailing bell flower of *Capanula isophylla*, an ideal subject for 'softening' the edges of the staging. The golden-leaved plant at the front is a helxine.

themselves with small flowers in many colours. They can be raised from cuttings or from seeds early in the year and are grown in the same way as the other greenhouse kinds.

IMPATIENS Busy lizzie
Temperature: 10° C (50° F).
Characteristics: Modern strains of impatiens are low-growing and compact. There are many to choose from, with flowers in brilliant colours, including red, pink, orange and white shades. Flowering is continuous throughout summer and well into autumn. The new Double Rosette impatiens are particularly attractive, with double flowers.
Cultivation: Sow the seeds in early or mid-spring and germinate in heat. Prick off seedlings direct into 9 cm (3½ in) pots and later move into final 12.5 cm (5 in) pots. Use peat-based or soil-based compost. Impatiens like light shade, plenty of moisture and high humidity.

PRIMULA
Temperature: 7–10° C (45–50° F). Certainly no higher than this.
Characteristics: Primulas are popular spring-flowering pot plants for the cool conservatory and are easily grown. The most popular are varieties of *P. obconica* with clusters of blooms in shades of red, pink, orange, blue, lilac and white. *P. malacoides,* popularly known as the fairy primrose, has tiers of star-shaped flowers in shades of red, mauve, pink, lilac and white. Yellow bell-shaped blooms are produced by the hybrid *P. × kewensis,* whose young leaves and flower stems are covered with a white powdery meal.
Cultivation: Sowing time for these primulas varies: sow *P. obconica* in early or mid-spring; *P. malacoides* in late spring or early summer; and *P. × kewensis* in late winter or early spring. Germinate in cool conditions: 15.5° C (60° F).Prick out seedlings into trays, then transfer to 9 cm (3½ in) pots. Final pot size is 12.5 cm (5 in). From early summer to early autumn grow in a cold frame, keeping the plants well ventilated, shaded and moist. Take into the conservatory in early autumn and provide airy cool conditions and good light. Keep the compost steadily moist in winter but avoid wetting the foliage. A peat-based compost is ideal for primulas.

SCHIZANTHUS Poor man's orchid
Temperature: 7–10° C (45–50° F). No higher as cool conditions needed.
Characteristics: This is an annual for the cool conservatory with

orchid-like blooms in a wide range of colours. Many strains are available from seedsmen. Plants can be flowered at various times of the year, but most people aim for winter or spring flowering.

Cultivation: For winter or spring flowering sow seeds in late summer and germinate in cool conditions such as a cold frame. Prick off into trays, and pot on into 9 cm (3½ in) pots. Split canes will be needed for support, or twiggy sticks. Grow in a well-ventilated cold frame and transfer to the conservatory in autumn. Pot on in late winter into 15 cm (6 in) pots. Use well-drained soil-based compost. Maintain cool airy conditions and take care with watering – the compost must not be kept wet.

SENECIO Cineraria

Temperature: 7–10° C (45–50° F). No higher as cool conditions needed.

Characteristics: Popular plants for the cool conservatory, varieties of *Senecio × hybridus* have large heads of daisy-like flowers on neat compact plants. Colours include pink. red, blue, purple and white, and flowering time is late winter and spring.

Cultivation: Sow seeds from mid-spring to early summer and germinate in a cold frame. Prick off into trays and then pot on into 9 cm (3½ in) pots. Final pot size is 12.5 cm (5 in). Use well-drained compost, soil based or peat based. Grow in a cold frame in well-ventilated, cool, shaded, moist conditions. Move into the conservatory in early autumn which should be cool and airy. Take care that the compost does not become too wet and avoid wetting the foliage.

SOLANUM Winter cherry

Temperature: 7° C (45° F).

Characteristics: The varieties of *Solanum capsicastrum* and *S. pseudocapsicum* produce red, orange or orange-red berries in the autumn and winter. Seedsmen offer many varieties such as 'Dwarf Red' and 'Red Giant'.

Cultivation: Sow seeds in late winter or early spring and germinate in the heated propagating case. Prick off into 7.5 cm (3 in) pots. Final pot size is 12.5 cm (5 in). Use well-drained soil-based compost. Pinch out growing tips of young plants to ensure bushy specimens. Grow out of doors for the summer and spray plants daily with water when in flower to ensure pollination and therefore a good crop of berries. Transfer to the conservatory in early autumn and provide airy conditions.

LONG-TERM PLANTS

These pot plants can be kept for several or many years, according to type.

BEGONIA

Temperature: 13–15.5° C (55–60° F).

Characteristics: Begonias can be had in flower at various times of the year. For winter there are the tuberous-rooted 'Gloire de Lorraine' hybrids in shades of pink, red, peach and white. The fibrous-rooted *B. semperflorens,* the wax begonia, can flower all the year round, and there are many varieties in shades of red, pink and white. There are many begonias with cane-like stems such as *B. corallina* with silver-spotted leaves and pink flowers from spring to autumn.

Cultivation: Begonias grow particularly well in peat-based composts. Be careful with watering, allowing the compost to partially dry out between applications. Provide a humid atmosphere, particularly when temperatures are high; ensure good light but shade from strong sunshine.

CLIVIA

Temperature: 7° C (45° F).

Characteristics: *Clivia miniata* is an evergreen perennial from Natal with long strap-shaped leaves and heads of orange funnel-shaped blooms in spring or summer.

Cultivation: An easily grown plant for the cool conservatory. Best growth is obtained by growing it in a soil bed, but it can also be pot grown. It does not like root disturbance as the roots are fleshy, so take care when potting on. Use a well-drained soil-based compost. Water normally in summer, but in winter allow the compost to almost dry out before watering. High humidity is appreciated in warm conditions and shade from strong sunshine.

CYMBIDIUM Orchids

Temperature: 10° C (50° F).

Characteristics: The cymbidium orchids are easily grown in the cool conservatory. There are many hybrids available, including miniatures, and they flower in winter and spring. Many colours are available.

Cultivation: Needs really good ventilation in summer. Shade from hot sun, spray the plants with water in warm conditions and liquid feed in summer. Keep the compost steadily moist. When the plants have really filled their pots, pot on in the spring, using a compost of equal parts bark and peat, with some pieces of charcoal added to keep it 'sweet'.

ERICA Heather
Temperature: 7° C (45° F).
Characteristics: The most popular of the greenhouse heathers is *E. ×
hyemalis,* a dwarf evergreen shrub with pink and white flowers in the
autumn and winter.
Cultivation: An ideal pot plant for the cool conservatory with airy
conditions. Plants are best kept out of doors for the summer, and
returned to the conservatory in early autumn. Keep the compost
steadily moist at all times, and apply liquid feeds in summer. Heathers
must have an acid or lime-free, peat-based compost. Allow them to
become slightly pot-bound before potting on.

FUCHSIA
Temperature: 4.5° C (40° F).
Characteristics: There are many hundreds of varieties of fuchsia in a
wide range of colours. They are shrubby plants and there are various
ways of growing them. Many can be grown as bush plants;
strong-growing varieties as standards or fan shapes; and pendulous
kinds in hanging baskets.

Fuchsias provide a continuous display throughout the summer.
Cultivation: Most people raise new plants each year and discard the
old plants. Soft cuttings root easily in spring or early summer, to
provide flowering plants the following year.

Plants can be kept for several years, though, and eventually make
large specimens. In this case they are rested over winter by keeping the
compost only barely moist. In the following spring they are started into
growth again by re-potting and increasing watering and temperature.
Prune back all shoots to within two or three buds of the base.

An impressive feature for the back wall of a conservatory is a fuchsia
trained to a fan shape, and maybe up into the roof area, too. This
should be planted in a soil bed and can remain there for many years.
Choose a strong vigorous grower such as 'Mme Cornelissen'.

Fuchsias grow well in peat-based composts and young plants should
be potted on until they are in 15–20 cm (6–8 in) pots. Airy conditions
are needed, plus shade from strong sun, plenty of water when in
growth, but far less in winter. Feed fortnightly in summer with a liquid
fertilizer.

HYDRANGEA
Temperature: 7° C (45° F).
Characteristics: Varieties of the garden hydrangea, *H. macrophylla,* are
excellent for the cool conservatory, producing their large mop-headed

blooms in the spring. The flowers may be pink or blue, but if you want blue flowers the plants should be grown in acid or lime-free compost.

Cultivation: Most people raise new plants each year by taking soft cuttings in the spring. Pot off rooted cuttings into 9 cm (3½ in) pots, and later pot on into 12.5 cm (5 in) pots. Pinch out the tips of the young plants. Keep plants in a well-ventilated cold frame for the summer, shading them and keeping the compost moist. In the autumn return them to the conservatory and pot on to 15 cm (6 in) pots. Keep compost only just moist in winter. Maintain airy conditions.

PELARGONIUM
Temperature: 7–10° C (45–50° F).
Characteristics: The regal pelargonium, varieties of *P. domesticum,* are popular pot plants for summer display. There are many varieties available in shades of red, pink, purple, mauve and white.
Cultivation: New plants are generally raised each year from cuttings taken in late summer, the old plants being discarded at the end of the season. Pot off rooted cuttings into 9 cm (3½ in) pots. In early spring pot on to 12.5 cm (5 in) pots. I prefer to use a well-drained, soil-based compost for regal pelargoniums. Basic conditions consist of plenty of light and sun, but keep shaded from very strong sunshine. Maintain a dry and airy atmosphere all year round. Water and liquid feed well in the growing season, but in winter keep the compost only slightly moist.

STRELITZIA Bird of paradise flower
Temperature: 7° C (45° F).
Characteristics: *Strelitzia reginae,* a native of South Africa, has flamboyant orange and blue flowers in summer, which are shaped rather like a bird's head, and large banana-like leaves. It grows to a height of about 1.5 m (5 ft).
Cultivation: Eventually the plant will need a large pot or tub, but the alternative is to grow it in a soil bed. When pot grown use a soil-based compost. This plant needs plenty of sun and very airy conditions. Feed well in the summer and water normally, but keep the soil/compost only slightly moist in winter. Young plants may take five years or more to flower, so be patient.

STREPTOCARPUS Cape primrose
Temperature: 7–10° C (45–50° F).
Characteristics: These are popular evergreen perennials which flower

in summer, bearing funnel-shaped or tubular blooms, purple-blue in the variety 'Constant Nymph', and in various colours in the John Innes hybrids.

Cultivation: In summer, shade from strong sun and provide high humidity. Water normally in spring and summer but in winter, when the plants are resting, keep the compost dryish. Overwinter in cool conditions.

FOLIAGE POT PLANTS

ASPARAGUS Asparagus ferns
Temperature: 10° C (50° F).
Characteristics: These African evergreen perennials are not true ferns, although they have ferny foliage, making a nice foil for brightly coloured flowering pot plants. Popular species are *A. plumosus; A. sprengeri;* and *A. asparagoides. A. sprengeri* is excellent for hanging baskets, or it can be allowed to trail over the edge of the staging. The other species can be trained to upright supports, such as pot trellis.
Cultivation: Provide a humid atmosphere in warm conditions, water normally all year round, and shade from hot sun. Regular feeding in summer is beneficial. A soil-based or peat-based compost is suitable.

BEGONIA
Temperature: 15.5° C (60° F).
Characteristics: There are many begonias, of tropical origin; with attractive foliage and all are evergreen perennials. Very popular with marbled, maple-like leaves are *B.* × 'Cleopatra' and *B.* × 'Tiger'. Others have red-flushed leaves, particularly on the undersides, like *B. erythrophylla* and *B. luxurians.* The most popular of all, though, are the iron-cross begonia, *B. masoniana,* with a deep purple cross in the centre of the leaves, and the multicoloured *B. rex.*
Cultivation: Provide high humidity in warm conditions, shade from direct sunshine, and feed once a fortnight in summer. Take care with watering – apply water only when the compost is drying out, and reduce further in winter. Grow in peat-based potting compost.

BROMELIADS Air plants, urn plants and earth stars
Temperature: 10° C (50° F).
Characteristics: The bromeliads, members of the pineapple family, are rapidly gaining in popularity and are destined to become as popular as cacti and succulents. Most of those we grow come from the tropical rain forests of South America, yet are very adaptable under cultivation

and are happy in low winter temperatures.

The air plants or atmosphereic tillandsias are epiphytic plants, growing on trees in the wild, and they absorb moisture through their leaves. They are small plants and very variable in habit: *T. caput-medusae*, *T. butzii* and *T. baileyi* are bulbous and have contorted leaves; *T. juncea* has rush-like leaves; *T. ionantha* forms contorted rosettes; *T. argentea* has fine silvery leaves; and *T. usneoides*, the Spanish moss, consists of green threads.

The ground-dwelling earth stars or cryptanthus are attractive bromeliads, with flat rosettes of striped, barred or mottled leaves. The popular epiphytic *Vriesia splendens* or a flaming sword, has a rosette of brown-banded leaves forming a 'vase' shape. The flower head consists of scarlet bracts and yellow flowers. Also forming 'vases' are *Guzmannia lingulata* with orange or red flower spikes, and *Nidularium fulgens*, with a bright red centre and a flower spike consisting of red bracts and violet flowers. Both are epiphytic.

The ornamental pineapple, *Ananas comosus* 'Variegatus', forms a wide rosette of narrow spiny leaves edged with cream. It is a ground dweller.

Other popular epiphytic bromeliads are *Tillandsia cyanea*, the pink quill, with a rosette of green leaves and a flower head of pink bracts and blue flowers; *Billbergia nutans*, queen's tears, which forms a clump of dark green grassy leaves and has green, pink and blue flowers; among pink bracts; and *Aechmea fasciata*, the urn plant, which forms a tall rosette of wide, grey-green banded leaves forming a 'vase', and has blue or lilac flowers among pink bracts.

Cultivation: The atmospheric tillandsias cannot be grown in pots – instead grow them on pieces of wood or on a 'plant tree' (see p. 33). Either gently wedge them into nooks and crannies, or tie into place with clear nylon thread. Lightly mist spray the plants daily in warm conditions, or once a week in cool conditions. Use rainwater or soft water. Provide good indirect light and plenty of fresh air.

The other bromeliads mentioned can be pot grown, using a well-drained peat-based compost.

Use small pots and pot on only when plants are pot bound. The epiphytic 'broms' could, alternatively, be grown on a 'plant tree'.

Keep the compost moist all year round but not wet. Provide very high humidity in warm conditions, but less in cool conditions. Provide good light but shade from sunshine. Those bromeliads which form water-holding 'vases' should have their vases filled with water. Replace it frequently to keep it fresh. Always use rainwater or soft water for bromeliads, as hard alkaline water can kill them.

The pineapple needs very good light, even direct sunshine, for the best leaf colour. It should be watered moderately, and in winter very sparingly – only enough to prevent the compost from drying out completely. Use clay pots and pot on every two years, using soil-based compost with extra peat.

CHLOROPHYTUM Spider plant
Temperature: 7° C (45° F).
Characteristics: *Chlorophytum comosum* 'Variegatum' is a popular evergreen perennial with green and white striped grassy leaves. Small plants develop on the ends of the old flower stems and will eventually form a cascade of growth. At this stage the plant is ideal for hanging containers or for the edge of the staging.
Cultivation: As it is a fast grower annual potting on may be necessary, using well-drained, soil-based compost. Water and feed well in summer; applying less water in autumn and winter. Shade from strong sun but ensure good light for best colour. Best conditions are warmth and humidity.

CISSUS Kangaroo vine
Temperature: 4.5° C (40° F).
Characteristics: *Cissus antarctica,* from Australia, is an evergreen climber with deep green glossy leaves. It is of modest stature and suitable for most conservatories.
Cultivation: Best grown in soil-based potting compost. The stems will need adequate supports. In summer provide high humidity and shade from strong sunshine – a good plant for a shady situation. Be careful with watering; allow the compost partially to dry out between applications. Feed fortnightly in the growing season. Pinch out the growing tips to encourage bushy plants. Prune back in late winter if the plant becomes too tall.

COLEUS Flame nettle
Temperature: 10° C (50° F).
Characteristics: Varieties of *Coleus blumei* have nettle-like leaves in many colours – some have leaves of one colour, others are multi-coloured. Most seedsmen offer a good range of varieties.
Cultivation: Most people treat coleus as short-term plants, discarding them at the end of the season and raising new plants from seeds in the spring. They can also be raised from cuttings. Good light is needed for the best leaf colour, but the plant should be protected from strong sun. High humidity should be provided in high temperatures. Water well in

A brick pillar provides support for *Mandevilla boliviensis*, while *acalypha wilkesiana roseomarginata* provides a purple background for the groups of pot plants, which include lilac and purple streptocarpus, orange aeschynanthus, red and yellow iresine, red-flowered hibiscus and *Asparagus sprengeri*.

summer and feed fortnightly. Pinch out the growing tips of young plants to ensure bushy specimens. Best grown in soil-based potting compost.

CORDYLINE
Temperature: 15.5° C (60° F).
Characteristics: From the tropical rain forests of India, *Cordyline terminalis* has large lanceolate leaves, bronzy red or purplish, but cream edged with pink when young. A most attractive variety is 'Tricolor' with cream, pink and red leaves.
Cultivation: Warm humid conditions are needed and, in summer, light shade. Water and feed well in the growing period, but reduce watering in winter. Use a soil-based potting compost.

DRACAENA
Temperature: 13° C (55° F).
Characteristics: The dracaenas are evergreen shrubs from tropical Africa and are very variable in habit. Most popular are *D. deremensis* and its varieties with green and silver (or white) striped, sword-shaped leaves. Palm-like is *D. marginata* from Madagascar, with long thin leaves. Variety 'Tricolor' is striped cream and pink.
Cultivation: Warmth, high humidity and in summer light shade are the main requirements. Feed and water well in the growing period; water more sparingly in winter.

FERNS
Temperature: 10° C (50° F).
Characteristics: The various kinds of ferns, generally with plain green but attractively cut leaves or fronds, are traditional conservatory plants and are used mainly as a foil for brightly coloured pot plants. Ferns were very popular with the Victorian-style conservatories. Ferns suitable for the minimum temperature of 10° C (50° F) include the adiantums or maidenhair ferns; *Asplenium bubliferum,* the spleenwort; *Cyrtomium falcatum,* the holly fern; *Dicksonia antarctica,* the tree fern; *Nephrolepis exaltata,* the sword fern, excellent for hanging baskets; *Platycerium bifurcatum,* the staghorn fern, ideal for hanging containers; and *Pteris cretica* and *P. tremula,* the table ferns.
Cultivation: Ferns should be protected from direct sun as it can cause the fronds to shrivel. High humidity is needed in warm conditions, plus an airy atmosphere. Keep the compost steadily moist all year round and feed fortnightly in summer. A peat-based potting compost is suitable for ferns.

FICUS Rubber plants and figs
Temperature: 15.5° C (60° F).
Characteristics: This is a diverse genus which contains trees, shrubs, climbers and trailing plants. The following are excellent plants for the conservatory: *F. benjamina,* the weeping fig from South East Asia, is a small pendulous tree with shiny oval leaves; *F. elastica* 'Decora' is the well-known rubber plant with large leathery deep green glossy leaves; *F. lyrata* is the fiddle-back fig from tropical West Africa, a tree with huge spoon-shaped leaves, deep glossy green; and *F. pumila,* the creeping fig from China and Japan, with small green heart-shaped leaves.
Cultivation: Requirements are straightforward: warm humid conditions, light shade from strong sun, regular feeding in summer, normal watering, but allow compost to dry out partially in winter. Use a soil-based or peat-based compost.

GREVILLEA Silk oak
Temperature: 4.5° C (40° F).
Characteristics: *Grevillea robusta* grows into a tall tree in its native Queensland and New South Wales, but under glass it makes a manageable specimen in a pot. It has ferny green leaves with silky undersides.
Cultivation: The silk oak likes an airy atmosphere and plenty of light, but shade from the hottest sun. Carry out normal watering but reduce in winter. Use an acid or lime-free soil-based compost and carry out annual potting-on as growth is rapid.

HEDERA Ivy
Temperature: 4.5° C (40° F); also suitable for unheated conservatory.
Characteristics: There are many varieties of our native *Hedera helix,* with plain green or variegated leaves. They can be grown as climbers but are very attractive when grown in hanging containers, or allowed to cascade over the edge of the staging. Larger-leaved ivies include *H. canariensis* 'Gloire de Marengo', the variegated Canary Island ivy.
Cultivation: These ivies are hardy plants so can be grown without heat. At any rate they prefer cool conditions, an airy atmosphere and humidity in warm weather. Keep the plants away from direct sun but give variegated ivies good light for best leaf colour. The greenleaved kinds are ideal for shady places. Carry out normal watering in summer but be very sparing with water in winter or roots may rot. Feed fortnightly in growing season. Use soil-based or peat-based potting compost.

MONSTERA Swiss cheese plant

Temperature: 15.5° C (60° F).

Characteristics: The popular *Monstera deliciosa* is a rain-forest climber from Mexico and various other parts of tropical America. To create a lush tropical effect in the conservatory there are few plants to equal it. The huge leaves are deeply cut and perforated, although young ones do not have this characteristic. Aerial roots are produced from the thick stems.

Cultivation: Monstera is best grown up a thick moss pole, into which the aerial roots will grow. Warm humid conditions are best together with shade from strong sun. Water moderately throughout the year and pot on regularly as growth is vigorous. Use a soil-based compost with extra peat. Feed fortnightly in the growing season.

PALMS

Temperature: 10–13° C (50–55 F).

Characteristics: No conservatory is complete without a palm and I would suggest choosing one of the larger kinds rather than dwarf palms. *Howea belmoreana* and *H. forsterana,* which grow in temperate forests of Lord Howe Island (in the South Pacific), have a well-divided feathery foliage held on tall stems. Not so tall is *Phoenix canariensis*, the Canary Island date palm, with stiff, prickly fronds.

Cultivation: Palms grow in good light to slight shade, but protect them from strong sunshine. Water well in the growing season but sparingly in winter when the plants are resting. A fortnightly feed in summer encourages good growth. Use a soil-based compost and pot on every two years until a large pot or tub is reached.

PHILODENDRON

Temperature: 15.5° C (60° F).

Characteristics: Like monsteras, palms and ficus, the philodendrons are, in my opinion, essential conservatory plants, creating a lush 'jungle' atmosphere. There are shrubby and climbing species and they come from the South American rain forests. They have large handsome leaves and many species produce long aerial roots from the stems. Some of my favourites include *P. bipinnatifidum,* with deeply cut leaves; the climbing *P. elegans,* also with deeply cut foliage; the climbing *P. erubescens,* with copper-flushed leaves; *P. hastatum,* a climber with shiny green foliage; the climbing *P. laciniatum,* with lobed leaves; and *P. scandens,* a climber with heart-shaped leaves.

Cultivation: The climbing kinds will need supports such as a thick moss pole into which they can bury their aerial roots. *P. scandens* is a good plant for a hanging basket. Warmth, high humidity and shade from the sun are the main requirements. Water normally in the season but apply far less in winter. Fortnightly feeds in spring and summer are beneficial. I use a compost of equal parts soil-based compost and peat.

SANSEVIERIA Mother-in-law's tongue
Temperature: 10° C (50° F).
Characteristics: The South African *Sansevieria trifasciata* is a remarkably tough plant, and has stiff, upright, sword-like leaves, rather fleshy. These are deep green with cross bands of lighter green. The more popular *S.t.* 'Laurentii' has yellow-edged leaves.
Cultivation: Provide very good light but shade from the hottest sun, and a dry atmosphere. Water with care – only apply when the compost is drying out. Allow to become slightly pot-bound before potting on, and use a well-drained soil-based compost.

TRADESCANTIA Wandering Jew
Temperature: 7° C (45° F).
Characteristics: Very common trailing evergreen perennials (but not to be despised for that), suitable for hanging containers and for cascading over the edge of the staging. There are several plain green and variegated varieties available; one of my favourites is *T. fluminensis* 'Quicksilver' whose leaves have bold white and green stripes.
Cultivation: Provide good light but shade from hot sun. Water normally in the growing period but keep much drier in winter, especially in low temperatures. Feed well in summer. Grow in soil-based or peat-based compost. Best to replace plants regularly with young specimens – cuttings root very easily in spring or summer.

ZEBRINA Wandering Jew
Temperature: 7° C (45° F).
Characteristics: Similar habit and uses to tradescantia. *Z. pendula* from Central America has silver-banded leaves, purple below. Better are the varieties 'Purpusii', green flushed with purple, and 'Quadricolor', leaves banded with pink, red and white.
Cultivation: This is the same as for tradescantia.

BULBOUS AND TUBEROUS PLANTS

BEGONIA
Temperature: 13° C (55° F).
Characteristics: The tuberous begonias make a highly colourful

display in the conservatory during the summer. They have large double flowers in a wide range of strong and pastel colours. There are also pendulous varieties which are excellent subjects for hanging baskets.

Cultivation: The tubers are started into growth in late winter or early spring. They are pressed into moist peat in a seed tray and ideally placed in a warm propagating case. Shoots will soon start to appear, at which stage the tubers are potted into 12.5 cm (5 in) pots of soil-based or all-peat compost. The top of each tuber must be level with the compost.

Feed once a fornight as soon as flower buds start to appear, and carry out normal watering. Shade from the sun.

The tubers can be kept for several years by drying off the plants in autumn, removing the tubers and cleaning them, and storing in dry peat in a frost-proof place.

CYCLAMEN
Temperature: 10° C (50° F).

Characteristics: The cyclamen, hybrids of *C. persicum,* are very popular autumn and winter-flowering pot plants which grow from tubers. There are many colours available including red, pink, purple, lilac, and white. Some varieties have beautifully marbled foliage, and in recent years some delightful miniature varieties have appeared on the market. Some cyclamen have scented blooms, and others are frilly.

Cultivation: Cyclamen can be raised from seeds sown in late summer. They are picked out into small pots, and potted on until eventually they are in 15 cm (6 in) pots. Peat-based potting compost gives good results. In the summer of the following year grow the young plants in a well-ventilated and shaded cold frame, and take into the conservatory in early autumn to flower. Bear in mind that cool airy conditions are needed at all times.

The tubers can be kept for many years. When the leaves start to die down dry off the plants and rest them in a cold frame. In late summer remove the tubers and re-pot into fresh compost. The top of the tuber must be above compost level. When watering cyclamen do not wet the centre of the plant or flower buds and leaf stalks may rot.

FREESIA
Temperature: 7° C (45° F).

Characteristics: Freesias are grown mainly for winter flowering and many have highly fragrant blooms. There are many colours available and flowers may be single or double. Ideal for the cool conservatory; high temperatures must be avoided.

Cultivation: Plant corms in late summer, about eight to a 15 cm (6 in) pot, using a soil-based compost and inserting them 2.5 cm (1 in) deep. Place in a cold frame and cover the pots with peat. Within six weeks growth should have started, at which stage the pots are moved into the conservatory. Provide good light and ventilation and water moderately. The plants will need supporting with thin twiggy sticks. After flowering start to reduce watering and eventually allow the compost to become dry, to give the plants a rest. In late summer, re-pot them ino fresh compost and start into growth again.

HIPPEASTRUM
Temperature: 10° C (50° F).
Characteristics: Hippeastrums produce huge trumpet-shaped blooms, from equally large bulbs. Spring is the usual flowering time, although blooms may appear in winter if conditions are fairly warm. Colours may be crimson, scarlet, pink or white, and some varieties are bi-coloured.
Cultivation: The bulbs can be started off in early winter if you have a warm conservatory, otherwise start them in late winter. Plant a single bulb in a 15 cm (6 in) pot, leaving the top half exposed. Use a soil-based potting compost. Re-pot bulbs every three years. When flowering has finished, start feeding with a liquid fertilizer. In late summer the leaves will start to die down. At this stage reduce watering to give the bulbs a rest, keeping the compost only just moist.

HYACINTHS
Temperature: Suitable for cool or unheated conservatory.
Characteristics: Hyacinths are hardy bulbs which will flower in winter or early spring under glass. Specially prepared bulbs will produce their blooms in time for Christmas. Most varieties are deliciously scented.
Cultivation: Bulbs should be planted in early autumn, including those specially prepared for very early flowering. Generally they are planted in bulb bowls, using bulb fibre, with the tips of the bulbs just showing.

After planting, the bulbs are placed in a cool shady position out of doors and covered with a 15 cm (6 in) layer of peat. They need to be kept in a temperature below 9° C (48° F). After about eight weeks, when roots and shoots have developed, transfer the bulbs to the conservatory and provide a temperature of 10° C (50° F). In the case of prepared hyacinths, the temperature can be increased to 15.5° C (60° F) when the flower buds have formed, to speed up flowering. Do not force bulbs again, but plant them in the garden.

NARCISSUS Daffodils

Temperature: Suitable for cool or unheated conservatory.
Characteristics: As with hyacinths, daffodils flower in the winter or early spring, and specially prepared bulbs bloom in time for Christmas. Daffodils are hardy so can be grown without heat if desired. There are many varieties to choose from, but still as popular as ever are the large, golden trumpet varieties.
Cultivation: This is the same as for hyacinths, the bulbs being planted in early autumn.

SINNINGIA Gloxinia

Temperature: 15.5° C (60° F).
Characteristics: Gloxinias are tuberous plants, hybrids of *Sinningia speciosa,* and produce their large bell-shaped blooms in summer, in shades of red, pink, purple and white, including bi-colours.
Cultivation: The tubers are potted in early spring, one per 12.5 cm (5 in) pot, with the tops only just below the surface of the compost. A temperature of 18–21° C (65–70° F) is needed to start them into growth, which could be provided with an electrically heated propagating case.

Water moderately during the growing season and liquid feed fortnightly. High humidity is recommended and shade from strong sunshine. The tubers are dried off in the autumn and stored in frost-free conditions for the winter.

TULIPS

Temperature: Suitable for cool or unheated conservatory.
Characteristics: All kinds of tulips make good pot plants for flowering in winter or spring in the unheated or cool conservatory. The specially prepared bulbs for Christmas flowering need more warmth, however. For the earliest blooms, choose the early-flowering varieties, with either single or double blooms.
Cultivation: This is the same as for hyacinths and planting time is early autumn.

ZANTEDESCHIA Arum lily

Temperature: 10° C (50° F).
Characteristics: *Zantedeschia aethiopica* is a popular South African plant which grows from a fleshy rhizome and produces in summer white flowers consisting of a large spathe and spadix. There are several other

species of arum lily including the yellow *Z. elliottiana* from the Transvaal, and the pink *Z. rehmannii* from Natal.

Cultivation: Plants can be potted in early spring and started into growth. Do not apply too much water at first, but increase as growth gets under way. In the summer feed fortnightly with liquid fertilizer. Arum lilies are dried off in the autumn to give them a rest; *Z. aethiopica* should not be treated in this way but kept moist all year round.

FRUITS

VITIS VINIFERA Grape vine

Temperature: Little or no heat needed in winter during the rest period.

Characteristics: The grape vine is the traditional conservatory fruit although when trained by the traditional method needs a fair amount of space and therefore is really only suitable for the medium-sized to large conservatory.

The most popular variety is 'Black Hamburgh' with black fruits, suitable for an unheated or slightly heated conservatory. If you prefer white grapes I can recommend 'Buckland Sweetwater', also suitable for an unheated or slightly heated conservatory. Needing the same conditions is 'Foster's Seedling', also a white grape. If you can provide a steady minimum temperature of 15.5° C (60° F) in the spring, and in autumn when fruits are ripening, you might like to grow the luscious, white-fruited 'Muscat of Alexandria'.

Cultivation: Traditionally a grape vine is grown on the back wall of the conservatory and the rod (the main stem) trained up the wall and into the roof area.

Start by planting a young vine in the winter in a well-drained soil bed or border. Ideally the soil should consist of good-quality loam with some well-rotted manure mixed in. If your soil is naturally poor it is a good idea to buy in some good loam or topsoil specially for the vine. Dig out the existing soil to a depth of about 60 cm (2 ft) and fill up with loam.

If you are growing more than one vine allow 1.2 m (4 ft) between them. The rod should be pruned back to a height of 60 cm (2 ft) above soil level after planting. The rod is trained to a system of horizontal wires, spaced 30 cm (12 in) apart up the wall and into the roof area. Select one strong new shoot in the spring and train it up the wires, removing any other shoots produced.

Side shoots will be produced from this rod, and when they are 60 cm (2 ft) long cut out the tips to prevent further growth. Then in the following winter they are pruned back to within one growth bud of their base. The length of the main rod may also need reducing, so again in winter cut it back to well-ripened wood.

Coming now to the second year, the new shoots produced in spring are trained horizontally to the wires. You may allow one or two to carry fruits in the second year, but remove most bunches to allow the vine to become well established. These side shoots will need stopping at two leaves beyond a bunch of fruits or they will grow exceedingly long.

In the second and subsequent years winter pruning consists of cutting back all side shoots to within one or two growth buds of their base.

The main rod should be untied in late winter and lowered to a horizontal position, supporting it with string attached to a roof wire. This will ensure that shoots break evenly all along the length of the rod. When shoots are being produced, re-tie the rod to its normal vertical position.

Let us now consider routine management of the grape vine. After the second year, one can allow two or three bunches of grapes to develop on each side shoot. In order to secure fruits, the flowers will need to be hand pollinated. All you do here is to draw your half-closed hand gently down each truss of flowers when they are fully open.

Many berries will be produced in each bunch and they must be thinned out otherwise they will not have sufficient space to develop. Thinning is done with a pair of fine-tipped vine scissors. Do not touch the berries with your hands or you will remove the waxy 'bloom'. Instead, during thinning steady the bunch with a thin, forked stick. As soon as the berries are the size of peas thin out the centre of each bunch. Further thinning will be necessary as the fruits swell – the aim being to leave each one sufficient space to develop to its full size.

Cut out the side shoots at two leaves beyond a bunch of fruits. These side shoots will produce shoots themselves (known as sublaterals) and these should be cut back to one leaf.

Very good ventilation is needed to prevent vine mildew. It is not necessary to provide artificial heat in the winter when the vines are resting but if possible provide heat in the spring when the vine is in flower. One relies on natural warmth in summer and autumn, when a minimum temperature of 13° C (55° F) is needed.

In warm conditions, damp down the conservatory to provide a humid atmosphere. However, the air should be dry when the vine is in flower and when the fruits are ripening. Water freely when the vine is in full growth but keep the soil only slightly moist when the plant is resting in the winter. Feeding is recommended in the summer: it is possible to buy a special vine fertilizer, otherwise use a general-purpose type.

PRUNUS PERSICA Peaches and nectarines

Temperature: Best to have no artificial heat in winter when plants are resting.

Characteristics: It is not difficult to produce luscious peaches and nectarines in a conservatory for they are hardy plants needing minimum artificial heat. I have grouped both fruits together for they are grown in exactly the same way, and in fact the nectarine is simply a smooth-skinned form of peach.

There are several varieties of peach available including 'Bellgarde', 'Dymond', 'Hale's Early', 'Peregrin' and 'Royal George'. Nectarine varieties include 'Early Rivers', 'Lord Napier' and 'Pine Apple'.

Cultivation: Peaches and nectarines can be trained to the shape of a fan on the back wall of the conservatory. For each tree you will need wall space of at least 1.8 by 1.8 m (6 by 6 ft).

Plant in a well-drained soil bed or border as for grape vines, and put up horizontal wires for training, spaced about 20 cm (8 in) apart.

I would advise buying a two-year-old fan-trained tree. You will probably need to buy from a specialist fruit grower. Planting time is late autumn or winter.

The newly planted tree is pruned very hard – the middle branch (which is growing vertically) is cut right back to the topmost side branches. The two lowest side branches should then be cut back lightly and tied in to one of the horizontal wires. All pruning cuts should be made just above dormant growth buds. Growth buds on peaches and nectarines are the long thin ones, whereas flower buds are fat and rounded in shape. Any remaining branches should now be pruned back to within a few centimetres of the main stem.

In the spring after this pruning many new shoots will be produced. They must be thinned out to avoid congestion. When carried out early enough, they can simply be rubbed out with the fingers. The aim is to leave only sufficient new shoots to form a fan-shaped system of the main branches. As these shoots grow tie them in to the wires, spacing them out as evenly as possible to form a neat fan shape. Never leave on the plant any shoots which are growing outwards. Shoots growing sideways, upwards or downwards are the ones to train.

We now come to the second winter. By this time the main branches should have produced several shoots along their length and made extension growth. You may find that some of the shoots have produced flower buds, and you can allow a few fruits to develop. The shoots should be tied in as flat as possible to the wires.

This is the basic method of training, but peaches and nectarines should be pruned annually in winter. Shoots which have carried fruits (and which are produced on the main framework of branches) are pruned back to new shoots. These replace the ones cut back and will carry fruits in the following sumer. Therefore, there is a constant succession of fruiting shoots.

Now to general care other than pruning. The trees will rest between late autumn and late winter and need little or no artificial heat. However, very airy conditions are required, so ventilate well whenever the weather is fine.

The buds will start to swell in the spring, a sign to reduce ventilation and to give a little artificial heat, maintaining, say, a temperature of 7° C (45° F), especially when the trees are in flower. During mild spells spray the trees with plain water twice a day. Damp down the floor in warm spells.

The flowers need to be hand pollinated to secure fruits, for there are no pollinating insects around early in the year. I use a soft paintbrush (the type used by artists), simply dabbing the centre of each flower in turn to distribute the pollen from one to another.

In the spring the trees will produce many new shoots and these should be thinned out to avoid congestion. You should leave sufficient at the base of the flowering/fruiting ones for fruiting next year and remove the rest.

The fruitlets will need thinning, too; leave two or three on each shoot, making sure they are evenly spaced. In the summer provide airy conditions, spray the trees twice a day. Fruit and shoot thinning should continue as necessary. I feed the trees with a high-potash fertilizer in the summer, using a dry fertilizer as a topdressing, pricking it into the surface of the soil.

When the fruits are ripening you should cease spraying, stop watering the soil, and give as much ventilation as possible. After harvesting the fruits, resume watering and spraying. Leaf fall occurs in the autumn, a sign to stop spraying. From now on reduce watering, applying only sufficient to keep the soil slightly moist.

In a temperate conservatory, summer colour provided by trained pot-grown bougainvilleas (*foreground*), large pot-grown coleus for coloured foliage, streptocarpus, and golden-leaved helxine. At the back of the group *Grevillea robusta* provides fresh ferny foliage.

CHAPTER 5

CHOOSING PLANTS FOR LIVING AREAS

As I see the situation, having talked to many people in recent years, a conservatory is purchased for one of two distinct reasons: primarily for growing plants, or mainly to provide living space for the owners.

In the first instance, where the prime consideration is growing plants, the conservatory owner is not faced with problems, for he or she will maintain an environment which is suited to the plants, but not necessarily to humans. He or she will be content to spend only comparatively short periods in the conservatory, tending and admiring the plants, and the unsuitable atmosphere (for humans) will not be a problem. In a plant conservatory a warm steamy 'jungle' atmosphere might be maintained, or very cool conditions in winter for plants which do not like too much heat.

However, where the conservatory is required for living in, the atmosphere must be suited to humans. Few people would want to work, play, relax, eat or entertain friends in an atmosphere reminiscent of a South American 'jungle', or at the other extreme wrapped up in winter clothing. Unfortunately, the atmosphere required by humans is not suited to a great many plants, so plants must be chosen with care, or cared for extra well if they are to survive. In a conservatory used for living in, plants are generally regarded as part of the decorations: they are used to enhance the overall decoration and furnishing schemes, in much the same way as houseplants are used. Quite possibly in a living area, therefore, plants would be used sparingly, the furniture playing a dominant part in the overall scheme of things.

THE IDEAL LIVING AREA

The ideal atmosphere to maintain in a conservatory used for living in is not easy to describe, for really it depends on the preferences of the owners. Only you know what is a comfortable temperature to maintain all the year round. However most people would maintain a steady temperature between 15.5 and 21° C (60 and 70° F). As with the rest of the house this would mean providing artificial heat in the autumn, winter and spring.

Such a temperature would be ideal for many plants, too, especially those of tropical and sub-tropical origin. For comfort, the level of atmospheric humidity should be low and indeed living areas generally have a dry atmosphere. One cannot live comfortably in an area of high humidity. Unfortunately, most plants do not like a combination of high temperatures and dry air. Tropical and sub-tropical plants, for instance, would make very poor growth and the leaves may shrivel and dry up, or turn brown at the edges. However, there are ways of ensuring plants have sufficient humidity without a moisture-laden atmosphere. And of course there are plants that actually thrive in warm, dry conditions. More about these later.

Now to the subject of light and shade. A conservatory must be fitted with blinds which can be rolled down in sunny weather, not only to reduce the glare of the sun, but also to help keep the temperature down in warm weather. A conservatory is like a greenhouse, of course: as soon as the sun shines the temperature rises, for the heat is trapped in the structure.

There is no problem with shade as far as plants are concerned for they, like humans, need shade from the sun and indeed would suffer if not protected. Many tropical and sub-tropical plants naturally inhabit shady places, such as forest floors. Details of blinds of various kinds are given in Chapter 1.

As already indicated, one of the problems in warm weather is trying to keep the temperature down to a comfortable level. Fortunately this is fairly easily achieved as most conservatories are fitted with plenty of ventilators and opening windows. And, of course the doors can also be left open. Also extractor or circulating fans could be installed. Such ventilation is also ideal for plants, as most need plenty of fresh air in warm weather. Ventilation equipment is recommended in Chapter 1.

These, then, are what I consider to be suitable living conditions. They are almost perfect for a great many plants, except for lack of humidity. So how can we ensure that our plants have sufficient humidity? If you have the time, spray them daily or twice daily with plain water, using one of the small mist sprayers intended for house plants. The moisture evaporating off the leaves will keep plants happy and will not affect the atmosphere.

Alternatively, plants could be stood on trays of gravel or pebbles, or even plunged to the pot rims in these materials. The gravel or pebbles should be kept permanently moist so that humid conditions are created around the plants. You will be providing a 'micro-climate' for the plants, while the atmosphere in the rest of the conservatory will be comfortable for living in (see Chapter 6).

CHOOSING PLANTS FOR THE 'LIVED-IN' CONSERVATORY

As already indicated there are many plants which can be grown in the 'lived-in' conservatory provided you are able to create a humid 'micro-climate' around them. All of the following can be recommended and are extracted from the descriptive lists in Chapter 4, so I will omit descriptions.

Plants which like warm conditions and high humidity

Shrubs: *Nerium* and *Tibouchina*.

Climbers: *Bougainvillea* and *Hoya*.

Flowering pot plants – short term: *Capsicum, Celosia, Impatiens* and *Solanum*.

Flowering pot plants – long term: *Begonia* and *Streptocarpus*.

Foliage pot plants: *Asparagus, Begonia,* Bromeliads, *Chlorophytum, Cissus, Coleus, Cordyline, Dracaena,* Ferns, *Ficus, Monstera,* Palms, *Philodendron, Tradescantia* and *Zebrina*.

Bulbous and tuberous plants: *Begonia* and *Sinningia*.

Plants which like warm conditions and which will thrive in a dry atmosphere

Shrubs: *Cestrum* and *Lantana*.

Climbers: *Plumbago*.

Flowering pot plants – long term: *Fuchsia* and *Pelargonium*. Cacti and succulents will also thrive in warm, dry conditions.

Foliage pot plants: *Sansevieria*.

Bulbous and tuberous plants: *Hippeastrum*.

WAYS OF DISPLAYING PLANTS

As with plants in the rest of the home, most people would want to display them atractively, and this means hiding the pots, for clay or plastic pots are not the most attractive objects.

There are available all kinds of ornamental pot holders, in which the pots are stood. The space between the pot and the side of the container

Fig. 11 Plants should ideally be displayed in groups as then they create more impact and their own micro-climate. There are many large floor containers or 'planters' available for displaying plants. The planter can be filled with peat and the pots plunged to their rims in this. It should be kept moist, when it will result in a moist atmosphere being created around the plants, which is particularly desirable for many tropical kinds in warm conditions. You must ensure that all plants need the same conditions. For instance, do not mix those which need warm and moist conditions with those which need cool and dry conditions.

could with advantage be filled with gravel or peat, which should be kept moist for those subjects which like a humid atmosphere.

For groups of plants there are many large floor containers available, fairly deep so that you can plunge pots to their rims in peat or shingle (Fig. 11). These generally come in plastic or wood. When grouping plants together make sure they all need the same conditions in respect of light, temperature and humidity. There is no doubt in my mind that plants grow much better when grouped, as they create their own micro-climate.

For trailing plants there are many attractive hanging containers available; for instance, in terracotta, or the more conventional hanging baskets. When buying hanging baskets for a living area make sure you choose those kinds which have a built-in drip tray to prevent the floor from becoming wet when watering.

An attractive way to display epiphytic (tree-dwelling) plants, like many of the bromeliads, is on a plant tree, the plants simply being tied on or gently wedged into place. Details of how to make a plant tree will be found in Chapter 3. The only problem with this in a conservatory for living in is that the plants have to be sprayed with water and this may wet the floor. However, it may be possible to stand the tree on a fairly large tray to catch any drips.

To summarize, when growing plants in the 'lived-in' conservatory, think in terms of growing them as houseplants, for essentially this type of conservatory is the same as a living room in the house.

THE SEASONAL LIVING AREA

If you cannot afford to maintain a comfortable temperature during the colder months of the year – which in the UK is usually late autumn, winter and the early part of spring – then the conservatory could be used for living in only between, say, late spring and early autumn.

There is usually sufficient natural warmth during this period of the year, when many people make maximum use of their conservatories; for instance, relaxing with a drink on a warm summer's evening, taking meals and for entertaining friends. In the spring and summer the conservatory is also a pleasant place to while away the time on wet days.

However, if the sun appears in winter the conservatory can become surprisingly warm even at that time of the year, for it traps the heat, so do not rule out the occasional 'coffee morning' for the winter amidst pleasant greenery and flowering pot plants.

I am thinking in terms of maintaining a minimum winter temperature of between 4.5° to 10° C (40° to 50° F). This will allow you to grow a good range of plants. With a minimum of 4.5° to 7° C (40° to 45° F), you will be maintaining what is correctly known as a 'cool conservatory'; and with a minimum of 10° C it will be an 'intermediate conservatory'. With a minimum of 10° C you will be able to grow a much wider range of plants than if you maintain a minimum of 4.5–7° C, but you will have to bear in mind that the heating bills will be considerably higher.

These minimum temperatures are not comfortable enough to live in for any length of time, at least I do not find them so. But such conditions are ideal for those plants which like cool conditions.

As far as plants are concerned, you should keep the air dry when conditions are cool, but as the weather warms up in the spring and summer many of the plants will appreciate some humidity, provided as outlined in 'The Ideal Living Area', page 81.

You may want to grow tropical and sub-tropical plants in your conservatory, but of course most will not tolerate the cool conditions in the winter. So between, say, autumn and late spring they should be kept in a warm room indoors and treated as houseplants. They will certainly benefit from a spell in the conservatory during the summer, and will welcome the better light and perhaps less stuffy conditions. It is surprising just how much growth many of them make when they have a 'holiday' in the conservatory.

There are many plants, though, that can be grown in the cool or intermediate conservatory all the year round, so you should never be short of attractive greenery and flowers even in the winter. Indeed, there are many pot plants for autumn, winter and spring flowering, and one should not forget, either, the hardy bulbs which bloom in winter and spring. In Chapter 4 I have described many plants suitable for the cool and intermediate conservatory, but for quick reference I have listed them below.

Some of the plants need a minimum of 10° C (50° F), while others will succeed with a minimum of 4.5–7° C (40°–45° F). I have lumped them all together here, so do check minimum temperature require-ments in Chapter 4.

Plants for the cool and intermediate conservatory

Shrubs: *Abutilon, Acacia, Brunfelsia, Callistemon, Camellia, Cestrum, Datura, Erythrina, Hibiscus, Lantana, Nerium, Rhododendron* and *Tibouchina.*

Climbers: *Bougainvillea, Clianthus, Hoya, Jasminum, Lapageria, Passi-flora* and *Plumbago.*

Flowering pot plants – short term: Annuals (hardy), *Calceolaria, Capsicum, Celosia, Chrysanthemum, Impatiens, Primula, Schizanthus, Senecio* and *Solanum.*

Flowering pot plants – long term: *Clivia, Cymbidium, Erica, Fuchsia, Hydrangea, Pelargonium, Strelitzia* and *Streptocarpus.*

Foliage pot plants: *Asparagus,* Bromeliads, *Chlorophytum, Cissus, Coleus,* Ferns, *Grevillea, Hedera,* Palms, *Sansevieria, Tradescantia* and *Zebrina.*

Bulbous and tuberous plants: *Cyclamen, Freesia, Hippeastrum,*

Here a pergola has been constructed to support *Bougainvillea* 'Miss Manila Hybrid'.

Hyacinths, *Narcissus,* Tulips and *Zantedeschia.*

Fruits: *Vitis vinifera* and *Prunus persica.* Grapes, peaches and nectarines are really better without heat in the winter, but *very* cool conditions would be acceptable, say, just frost-free.

THE UNHEATED CONSERVATORY

With the ever-rising cost of heating, many people are finding that they simply cannot afford to heat a conservatory. However, even a 'cold' conservatory, as it is correctly termed, can still be used as a seasonal living area as soon as the weather warms up sufficiently in the spring. You should be able to make good use of the conservatory throughout the summer months and into the autumn.

Of course, the great problem is that you will not be able to keep tender plants in the conservatory over the winter for they will become frosted. Again the solution is to keep them in a warm room indoors over the winter.

You should be able to have a good summer display of such plants as fuchsias, pelargoniums, streptocarpus, celosias, impatiens and others. In the autumn you could have a fine display of greenhouse chrysanthemums.

The cold conservatory is an ideal place to grow grapes, peaches and nectarines as they do not need heat in the winter.

But having ensured summer and autumn colour and interest, we now need to consider how to keep the conservatory interesting and colourful during the winter and spring. It is, of course, a case of furnishing it with hardy plants.

Camellias are an excellent choice for the unheated conservatory, growing them in tubs and keeping them out of doors for the summer. Depending on variety, they will flower in winter or spring. The hardy annuals grown in pots will flower in the spring in an unheated conservatory and a superb display they make, too. Sadly, they are not often grown by amateur gardeners for this purpose, and yet they are so easy.

Hardy bulbs will flower in spring – hyacinths, narcissus and tulips, and their blooms should be perfect as they will be well protected from the weather.

There are plenty of hardy foliage plants which could be grown in pots and taken into the cold conservatory for the winter. I am particularly fond of *Fatsia japonica,* an evergreen shrub with huge hand-shaped glossy green leaves. Eventually it makes quite a large specimen, so if it becomes too big you could either plant it out in the garden or grow it in a large tub, provided you are able to move it.

One should not forget the many ivies, for trailing over the edge of the staging, for hanging containers or for growing as climbers up canes, wire hoops, etc. These are described in Chapter 4. In cold conditions you may find that the foliage of some of them changes colour, perhaps taking on reddish or purplish tints – this is quite natural.

To my mind among the best plants for flowering in the cold conservatory during winter and spring are the alpines, like saxifrages, alpine primulas and spring-flowering gentians. These are grown in pans of gritty soil-based compost and taken into the conservatory as they are coming into flower. For the rest of the year they can be kept in a well-ventilated cold frame.

When temperatures are low in the autumn and winter, and into spring, you must keep the atmosphere as dry as possible in the cold conservatory. Do not splash water around, water plants with care to keep them only moderately moist, and above all provide plenty of ventilation, except during gales or foggy weather. Dry airy conditions will ensure your plants thrive instead of rotting off.

CHAPTER 6

CARING FOR THE PLANTS

To ensure your plants flourish, lavish care and attention on them and make sure the basic techniques of watering, feeding, potting, pruning and so on are carried out correctly. Here is a basic guide to routine plant care throughout the year.

WATERING

This aspect of plant care causes more problems with the newcomer to gardening than any other. He or she is often uncertain of when to water plants and how much water to apply. Yet this technique has to be mastered, for if plants are kept too wet they are liable to suffer root rot and eventually they die. If plants are given insufficient water they will be under considerable stress and will not grow and flower well.

You will find that I have indicated in Chapter 4 water requirements for the plants. Generally, although it does not apply to all plants, more water is needed in the growing period (spring and summer for most) than in the rest period (autumn and winter).

Let us, therefore, start with ascertaining when to water plants in the growing period. Bear in mind that with most subjects we do not want the compost to dry out too much during this period. I would advise testing the compost or soil for moisture with a finger. Press a finger into the surface and if it feels dry on top, but moist below, then apply water. If the surface is moist or even wet, do not water. When watering do not give a 'quick splash', but fill the space between the compost surface and the rim of the pot with water. This will ensure the compost is moistened right the way down to the bottom of the pot.

The soil in a bed or border can be tested in the same way: apply sufficient water to penetrate to a depth of about 15 cm (6 in), which means giving about 27 litres per square metre (4¾ gallons per square yard).

When watering in the autumn and winter, during the plants' rest period, and when conditions are cooler, I have advised in Chapter 4 to keep the compost or soil only slightly moist, to water more sparingly or to reduce watering for many of the plants. How can we put this into practice? Again I would advise testing with a finger, pushing it well down into the compost. If the compost is dry on the surface, and feels dryish but not completely dry lower down, water can be applied, again filling the space between the compost surface and the rim of the pot. Then leave well alone until the compost is drying out again. It is far better not to water if in doubt, than to keep the compost too wet. Far better to leave the plant for a few more days, unless it is wilting.

FEEDING

Potting composts supply plants with foods for a certain period, generally several months, depending on the type of fertilizer used in the mix. Therefore newly potted plants do not need feeding. The time to start is when the roots have permeated the new compost which, in practical terms, is about two months. The same applies to plants which have been potted on to larger pots.

Then feeding can be carried out about once a fortnight for most subjects, but only in the growing season – spring and summer – and perhaps early autumn if plants are still making growth. Do not feed in late autumn, winter and early spring, when most plants are resting, for they will not use the fertilizer and an excess of foods can build up in the compost, which can be harmful.

There are various ways of feeding potted plants, but the most popular is to apply a liquid fertilizer. There are many proprietary brands available, but for conservatory plants I would suggest using a houseplant fertilizer. Some of these are based on seaweed.

Another way of feedng potted plants is to use fertilizer tablets, again specially formulated for houseplants. These are about the size of an aspirin tablet and are simply pushed into the compost, where they release plant foods over a period of weeks.

There are various ways, too, of feeding permanent plants in soil beds or borders. I like to apply a dry general-purpose fertilizer in mid-spring and lightly prick it into the soil surface. Then in the summer, if I feel that plants need a boost, I water them with a general-purpose liquid fertilizer, say about once a month. Plants in soil beds do not need regular feeding as with potted plants, as foods are not leached out so rapidly.

Plants should not be fed if the compost or soil is dry – water it first and them feed when the plants are fully charged with water.

It is most important to apply fertilizers strictly according to the instructions on the packet or bottle, for you could harm plants by applying too much, or too strong a solution.

Halls Silverline conservatories have aluminium framework, available as natural or with a white polyester finish, and feature double sliding doors and curved eaves. White wrought-iron furniture is a perfect choice for this conservatory, which has been skilfully merged into the garden.

DAMPING DOWN

I have emphasized throughout the book that many plants need a humid atmosphere, particularly in warm conditions. The lower the temperature the drier the air must be. The technique known as damping down provides atmospheric humidity and involves sprinkling the floor and staging with water – perhaps twice a day in very warm conditions, morning and evening.

However, damping down is not a practical proposition for conservatories which are used for living in for not only does it create too much humidity for comfort, but you may not want to wet the floor. So it is usually reserved for conservatories which are used for the cultivation of plants.

However, plants in living areas still need humidity, but it can be localized. For instance, potted plants could be stood on shallow trays filled with gravel, shingle or one of the horticultural aggregates. These materials are kept moist to create a humid atmosphere around the plants, but make sure the pots do not stand in water or the compost will become too wet.

Another method is to plunge pots to their rims in peat, shingle or horticultural aggregate and to keep these moist, In this instance you will, of course, need deep containers or 'planters'.

Another method of ensuring humid conditions around plants is to spray them daily or twice daily in warm conditions with plain water. Use a small mist sprayer for this – the type designed for indoor use. It is best, though, not to spray flowers, and never spray plants with hairy or woolly leaves, or cacti and succulents. Use soft water or rainwater for spraying plants, for 'hard' or alkaline water can result in unsightly white marks on the leaves.

VENTILATING

Plants as well as people need fresh air at all times and therefore adequate ventilation is needed all the year round. Ventilation also helps to reduce the temperature, particularly necessary in hot weather; and it helps to reduce humidity, which is important for plants growing in cold or cool conditions.

The amount of ventilation you provide should be consistent with maintaining the desired temperature – there is no point in providing a great deal of ventilation if it results in the temperature dropping to an unacceptable level for plants and people.

The way to ensure effective ventilation is to open the roof ventilators and also the side ventilators or louvres. Because warm air rises, it will rise and escape through the roof, drawing in cool air through the side ventilators.

SHADING

Again adequate shading is needed by both plants and people in the spring and summer. Without shading the leaves and flowers of plants can be badly scorched during periods of strong sunshine. Shading also helps to keep temperatures down to an acceptable level in hot weather.

For plants, shading should ideally only be used when the sun is shining and removed during dull periods so that they receive maximum light, and this is best achieved by the use of roller blinds (see Chapter 1).

As you will have seen in Chapter 4, plants vary in the amount of light or shade needed. Some like plenty of sun, including many cacti and succulents, while others should be well shaded from strong sunshine, including ferns and many of the tropical plants. For the sake of convenience it would perhaps be better to grow in your conservatory only plants which need to be shaded – that is, if it is used as a living area.

Remember that in autumn and winter plants need all the light they can get, so shading should not be used during these seasons – and I doubt if you will need it either.

POTTING

Most plants make much better growth if they are potted on (Fig. 12) regularly into larger pots. If allowed to become pot-bound, when the compost is tightly packed with roots, growth will slow down considerably. Also, the compost will dry out very rapidly so you will be forever watering, and there is the risk plants will suffer stress from lack of moisture.

Having said this, there are some plants that should not be potted on regularly, either because they do not like root disturbance or because they have only a small root system; therefore small pots are adequate for their needs. I have indicated this where applicable in my list of plants in Chapter 4.

If plants need potting on annually this should preferably be carried out in spring as growth is commencing. Some plants will need further potting on during the summer and maybe early autumn, particularly

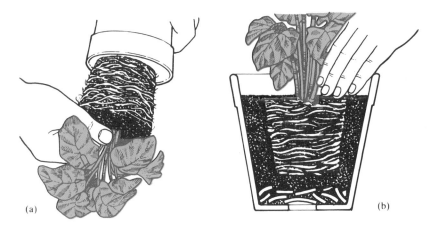

(a) (b)

Fig. 12 To ensure steady and healthy growth most conservatory plants need potting quite regularly into larger pots. This should normally be done before the present pot is tightly packed with roots, so periodic checking of the rootball will be necessary (a). If the plant needs moving on (b), either put it into the next size of pot or move it on two sizes. There should not be a large volume of compost around the roots or this will remain very wet and could lead to root rot. When we come on to larger pots – say over 15 cm (6 in) in diameter, it is advisable to use drainage material in the bottom, such as a layer of broken clay flower pots or 'crocks'.

short-term pot plants. Try to avoid potting on in winter when plants are resting, for they will not make new roots into the fresh compost and consequently the compost may remain too wet. The roots may then rot.

To ascertain whether or not a plant needs potting on, you will need to inspect the roots. To do this, turn the pot upside down and tap the rim on the edge of a table or bench to loosen the rootball, and slide off the pot. If there is a mass of roots then pot on; but if a large volume of the compost has no roots through it, return the plant to its present pot.

If possible pot on into the next size of pot, for example from a 12.5 cm (4 in) pot to a 15 cm (6 in) pot. However, more vigorous plants can with advantage be moved on two sizes – for instance, from a 10 cm (4 in) pot to a 15 cm (6 in) pot.

The trend these days is to dispense with drainage material in the bottom of the pot. But I feel that for plants which like very well drained conditions drainage should be provided; and I also think it is necessary when we come onto larger pots – say over 15 cm (6 in) in diameter. The traditional drainage material is broken clay flower pots, known as 'crocks'. A large piece is placed over the drainage hole and then a layer

Baco Garden Rooms, in aluminium with acrylic bronze finish, are available in three standard lengths and two widths and any of these may be extended at a later date, using Baco extensions.

of smaller pieces placed over this. Cover with a thin layer of rough peat or leafmould, followed by a layer of compost which should be firmed. Place the plant in the centre and fill in with compost, firming all round with your fingers. You should ensure the top of the rootball is slightly covered with fresh compost, and there must be a space between the final compost level and the rim of the pot to allow for watering. This can be about 12 mm (½ in) for small pots and up to 2.5 cm (1 in) for larger pots.

After potting water in the plant with a rosed watering can to settle the compost around the roots.

Plastic pots are often used today, but for plants which like very well drained conditions and dryish compost, I prefer clay pots. I also use clay pots for large plants as they are heavier and more stable.

Now let us take a look at suitable potting composts. You will see in Chapter 4 that some plants are best in soil-based compost, this being the traditional John Innes potting compost, which is well drained and aerated. It is readily available from garden centres and consists of loam (soil), peat and sand, plus John Innes base fertilizer and chalk. John Innes potting compost No. 1 is used for the initial potting of young plants, such as seedlings and rooted cuttings. When potting on use JIP2 which contains twice the amount of fertilizer. When potting on larger plants – for instance, shrubs which are being grown in large pots or tubs, use JIP3 which contains three times the amount of fertilizer.

Other plants are happy in the more modern soilless or peat-based composts and again I have indicated this where appropriate in Chapter 4. These consist of peat with fertilizers. They are ideal for plants which like plenty of humus and moist conditions, for peat-based composts are inclined to hold more moisture then soil-based types. One needs to be careful to prevent keeping all-peat composts too wet.

There are peat-based composts specially formulated for houseplants and these would be suitable for conservatory plants, too. General-purpose soilless composts would also be suitable. You will find a good range in garden centres.

If you are growing plants which dislike lime or chalk in the soil, such as rhododendrons and camellias, you must use a lime-free or ericaceous compost. It is possible to buy soil-based or soilless acid potting composts.

PRUNING

I have indicated how to prune plants where applicable in Chapter 4, so here I will consider only the basic rules.

Firstly, always use really sharp secateurs for it is essential to make clean cuts. These heal very much quicker and better than ragged cuts made with blunt secateurs and are therefore less liable to be infected by diseases.

When you are cutting back branches or shoots, always cut just above a growth bud; not so far above that you leave a portion of stem, which will only die back to the bud and not so close that you damage the bud, which may then come into growth, Growth buds are situated in the axil formed between the base of a leaf stalk and the stem.

If you have to remove large branches from, say, a shrub, all pruning cuts over 2.5 cm (1 in) in diameter should be 'painted' with a proprietary pruning compound to seal them and prevent the possible entry of diseases.

Many plants do not need regular pruning, but you should always keep an eye open for any dead or dying shoots and cut these back to live wood.

Removal of dead flowers is a form of pruning and is certainly recommended, not only for the sake of tidiness but to prevent the disease grey mould or botrytis from infecting the dead flowers, from where it could spread to healthy tissue.

Another form of pruning is the technique known as 'stopping' or 'pinching'. This is where the growing tip of a young plant is pinched out or cut out to encourage side shoots to develop, so creating a bushy specimen. Plants like bush fuchsias and chrysanthemums are stopped or pinched when they are about 15 cm (6 in) high. Sometimes the resultant side shoots are stopped to create really well-balanced plants.

CONTROLLING PESTS AND DISEASES

In a conservatory used for living in one cannot go around spraying everything with a pressure sprayer as one would in a greenhouse, in order to control pests and diseases. Nor can one use smoke cones for pest and disease control, although these are ideal for the conservatory devoted to plants.

It would be more practical to use an aerosol houseplant pest killer with a wide spectrum of activity. One such will eradicate pests like greenfly, red spider mites, whitefly, scale insects, mealy bugs and thrips. To date there are no fungicides specifically for use in the home, so if any of your plants are infected with common fungal diseases such as mildew and grey mould (botrytis), take them outdoors and spray them thoroughly with benomyl fungicide. When dry take them back inside.

GENERAL HYGIENE

The conservatory which is devoted purely to growing plants will need thoroughly cleaning out at least once a year. Due to frequent damping down of floor and staging, and perhaps spraying the structure and plants with a hosepipe to create humidity in hot weather, green algae and slime build up on all surfaces.

Ideally the conservatory should be completely emptied of plants and the inside scrubbed out with a horticultural disinfectant. Clean the glass, framework, staging and floor. The green algae which build up in the glass overlaps can be removed by inserting a thin plastic plant label between the panes and then flushing out with a hosepipe. Finally forcefully wash down the structure with the hosepipe. Clean the outside, too, in the same way.

Shingle, gravel and so on, on benches and staging, can be washed in a sieve, using a hosepipe. This will get rid of any soil or compost which has washed down into it.

Of course, you cannot treat a living area in this way, but still it will need cleaning, perhaps not so much framework, but certainly the glass. This must be kept clean at all times to allow maximum light transmission. There are horticultural glass cleaners available which not only remove green algae and grime, but leave the glass sparkling. The overlaps between the panes of glass can again be cleaned out with the help of a thin plastic plant label.

APPENDIX

A SELECTION OF CONSERVATORY MANUFACTURERS

Baco Leisure Products Ltd, Windover Road, Huntingdon, PE18 7EH.

Banbury Homes and Gardens Ltd, P.O. Box 17, Banbury, Oxfordshire, OX17 3NS.

Crittall Warmlife Ltd, Crittall Road, Witham, Essex, CM8 3AW.

Edenlite Products (Eden), Wern Works, Briton Ferry, Neath, West Glamorgan, SA11 2JS.

Florada Garden Products, Dollar Street House, Dollar Street, Cirencester, Gloucestershire, GL7 2AP.

Halls Homes and Gardens Ltd, Church Road, Paddock Wood, Tonbridge, Kent, TN12 6EU.

Marley Buildings Ltd, Peasmarsh, Guildford, Surrey, GU3 1LS.

Robinson's of Winchester Ltd, Robinson House, Winnall, Winchester, Hampshire, SO23 8LH.

INDEX